A Soldier's Life

LOU W. GERAETS

Copyright © 2012 Lou W. Geraets

Published by BMS Books
An imprint of Business Media Services Limited
5 High Street,
P.O. Box 6215, Whakarewarewa
Rotorua 3010
New Zealand
Tel: 64-7-349 4107
Email: ms@bms.co.nz
Web site: www.bms.co.nz
All rights reserved.
Published: September, 2012

ISBN: 978-0-473-22111-9

Also published in colour as 'My Life – the Meanderings of Pop Knill
ISBN: 978-0-473-22110-2

DEDICATION

To Sandra – without her this story would not have the meaning it has.

CONTENTS

	Acknowledgments	i
	Introduction	ii
1	Earlier Years – Family Lines	1
2	Childhood Years – Shaddock Street, Mt Eden	18
3	The Knill Family, My Working Life Begins	33
4	The War Years, Pop – Trooper 21939	59
5	End of War Years and a Return to Shaddock Street	137
6	Courting, Marriage, Homes and Families	141
7	Working Life After the War	158
8	Holidays, Automobiles, the T.A.B. and Cigarettes	169
9	Retirement	185
10	The More Recent Years - Pop's Legacy, Nan	191
11	Final Words	194
	About the Author	196
	Index	197

ACKNOWLEDGMENTS

The contributions made to this story by Cherie D'bois in Australia and Toni Evans in Auckland are very much appreciated. Thanks also to Yvonne McLaughlin for her proof reading. And to Mike Smith from Business Media Services Ltd for his guidance and putting up with continual changes.

Where possible we have sought and received permissions to publish photographs and maps. Where it has not been possible to contact or obtain permission, we have acknowledged the source. Thank you very much to all those who have given permission to utilise their material.

For those who had to put up with detailed questioning – your patience will hopefully be rewarded.

I wish to acknowledge Pop's openness and willingness to write his story. We have completed what we set out to do and may well have added a little bit more to the original intention.

INTRODUCTION

This is a story that Charlie Knill (Pop) wanted to tell.

Life goes on, and goes on quickly. Memories remain a part of our lives. Some memories we share and some we hold privately, sometimes waiting for the right time to tell them. Sometimes we never get the chance or memories die with us never to be shared.

This is a remarkable tale. Not remarkable in the sense that it is an account of world conquering feats, but remarkable in the sense that it is a human story. It tells of a long life, still remembered by he who lived it, 96 years on and unconquered. Not much of the tale has been written down elsewhere. The story has been recalled and recounted in conversations over the decades and more so by Pop during 2011.

Most of the words are Pop's but I have interpreted them in some cases. The reader will notice break outs where I have added my own thoughts. These have been deliberately placed in italics to emphasis they are my questions and conclusions rather than necessarily being those of Pop.

Historical accuracy is not the prime focus of this tale, although all those involved in the process have tried to ensure this as much as possible. Pop called it "The meanderings of Charlie Knill" so that we can share his life's journey with him.

Joys and heartaches are shared on the following pages.

Lou W Geraets

CHAPTER 1

EARLIER YEARS – FAMILY LINES

The world into which I was born was very much different than the world I live in today. I was born on the 6th April, 1916, the son of Charles and Gladys (nee Golding) Knill. My father, Charles Alfred Abraham Knill, was born in 1889 in Southampton, Hampshire, and immigrated to New Zealand from Australia where he spent a few years with his father. Also named Charles Alfred, my father's dad was born in 1864 in Dartmouth, Devon, England. My grandfather was married to Alice Knill (nee Arruis). In 1891 they were living in St Petrox, Devon. My farther Charles, married Gladys in Auckland, where they first met shortly after he arrived here from Australia. Our first home was located in Surrey Crescent, Grey Lynn towards the top of Chinaman's Hill.

The marriage certificate of Charles and Gladys, 1911.

Back in 1916 life was a lot different than it is today. No smooth bitumen roads, acrylic painted houses or brightly lit car sales yards. The Cameo Picture Theatre which sat at the top of Chinaman's Hill has long since disappeared as has the Adams Bruce speciality ice cream and chocolate shop. Early memories of home, and the Grey Lynn area, are ones of bush-clad hills, where kids rummaged and played their games. Where you could get lost and wander off home late even if trouble awaited you on your return.

In 1883 one of Auckland's first major residential developments took place in Grey Lynn after James Williamson and Thomas Grummer acquired the 314 acre Surrey Hills farm. In 1898 the area was renamed Grey Lynn, after Sir George Grey, who had been the parliamentarian for Newton and twice Governor of New Zealand. In 1914 Grey Lynn was amalgamated with Auckland City. This was an industrious area with slaughterhouse, tanneries, fellmongeries and a soap and candle making operation.

The population of Grey Lynn in 1926 was approximately 11,000 when Auckland's population was 200,000. A high percentage of residents were hard working and striving to own their own homes.
(Source – www.customresidential.co.nz/neighbourhoods/grey-lynn-westmere/)

In the early 1920s and post-World War I, development in housing around the area offered some security for Grey Lynn residents, providing additional job and housing opportunities. However the Great Depression was looming and for many families 'struggle' was a word they understood.

Our early family life was 'poor'. Not always knowing what there was to eat except that it was likely to be bread or a vegetable from the garden. My parents, Charles and Gladys, went about doing what they could to provide for our family of seven (later to be nine).

The first three or four years were spent living in a small weatherboard bungalow in Surrey Crescent. It is difficult to remember much of these early years at our first home but two recollections stand out for me. The first was that life seemed to offer only hard work and 'poor' conditions, day after day, leaving little room for dreaming of life's comforts. Living poor meant always feeling, consciously or unconsciously, of being in a constant state of 'wanting and needing'. Bread being the staple diet apart from a few home grown vegetables. There was little to spread on our bread and every slice was counted. Treats were rare.

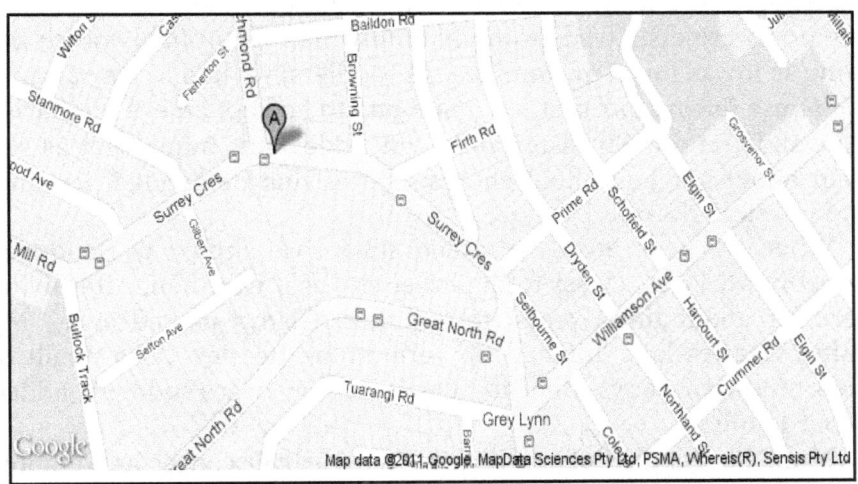

The first family home was located in Surrey Crescent in Grey Lynn. (Source: Google Maps)

The second memory I have is of a murder that happened in the bush land of Chinaman's Hill. It is hard to recall the details at four years of age but murders are dramatic events which even young ones can remember. I certainly did. Especially this murder since the prime suspect was believed to be a detective's son. Such scandal probably helped this memory stick in my brain, young as I was.

In researching Auckland murders which had occurred at this time, it seems that this murder Pop relates to may well have involved the murder of the Ponsonby Postmaster Augustus Braithwaite in 1920. Dennis Gunn was convicted of the murder and was executed by hanging. This was to be the first conviction in New Zealand based on the forensic science evidence of fingerprinting.
(Source – www.executedtoday.com/2009/06/22/1920-dennis-gunn-fingerprint-evidence/)

Family Lines

I was the first born to Charles and Gladys, followed some 24 months later by Alma. After 18 months or so Jack arrived, followed in turn, by Irene and finally by Ernie. Although only a child, the earliest years at home I remember as being uneventful but secure and contented. Not a whole lot of outward expressions of love and emotion were displayed, however family life was probably much the same as it was for many families. As toddlers, we had to stay around the house during our first few years just to be kept an eye on in case we wandered off. My sister and I got under our mum's feet as she went about her household chores; chores that demanded her time and physical effort.

When we were about to attend school we shifted to Shaddock Street in Mt Eden, closer to the inner city as it was then. After living here for about three years, my mother, Gladys passed away. My father Charles later hitched up with Annie Beesley. As a result of their union, two boys, Billy and Owen Beesley, were suddenly added to our family.

Mum Gladys died of yellow jaundice (or liver cancer as we know it today) in 1924 when I was only eight years old. Dad Charles often cried in the night after Gladys died. Many a tear Charles shed. The effect Gladys' death had on him was obvious to see although we didn't appreciate how hard it was on him at the time. Charles did not forewarn us of Gladys' true condition believing that his children were still too young. Up until her death I did not really appreciate how bad mum's condition really was. Mum's coffin was brought back to the family home and placed in the front dinning room until the burial. Candles were lit and placed around the casket and around the room.

Dad Charles seemed to have done all the crying as we children didn't do much of that, being so young and wanting to play and not really understanding what it was all about. Mum Gladys was interred at Waikumete Cemetery on the 5th September, 1924.

Was death something families openly discussed in these days, or was death seen as a sad thing to be kept under wraps because of personal attitudes and behaviours? The way Pop tells it, death evoked sadness however death wasn't explained to children, you handled it mostly on your own and that could be by not questioning it.

My sister, Alma, did what she could to help father with the household chores even though she was so young. Making beds, doing dishes, cleaning and sweeping, she tried to help with. The other siblings left her to it not making much effort to share the load even though Charles had said that the children must help Alma. At such a young age this must have been a big responsibility and probably something Alma took up naturally as I always remember her as a gentle, caring lady. I got on well with my younger sister. Alma continued undertaking these chores until a young woman thought to be Gladys' sister's daughter appeared in the household. As children, we did not know where she had come from. Shortly after the young ladies arrival her parents visited our home.

At some point an argument developed, probably relating to father Charles having overworked our new housekeeper. As a result of this episode the young lady soon left and our family was back at square one with no one except Alma keen to look after the basic household chores. Whatever arrangements had been agreed to, as to the young ladies responsibilities for running the household, things did not work out and she was now gone. Losing the housekeeper caused further hardships and misunderstandings within our family just when we were struggling with the recent loss of our mother. Charles tried to handle the situation by saying to us,

"Never mind, we shall get another"

It was some four years later that Charles met Annie Beesley. They got together in 1928 and then married in 1930. Charles and Annie proceeded to set up house together at Shaddock Street. Looking back, I believe that Annie was looking primarily for security. Annie (Beesley) had been previously married and brought with her two sons, Billy and Owen. I remember Billy and Owen being noticeably different in physical stature and wondered if different fathers were involved. At some point in this relationship Annie expressed the desire to have more children however this did not find favour with my father. Times were difficult for me and I found it hard to get on with my stepmother. I recall how Annie tried to match me up with Edie's sister Pearl (Edie was married to Annie's son Billy). However

Pearl was not my type and I resisted any encouragement. At least she tried, even though I never really understood her motivations.

Annie had a habit of throwing black coal as a way of demonstrating her anger, not only at Charles, her husband, but also at me. Provoked one day, I threatened my stepmother with a knife and that was enough to stop coal throwing in its tracks. This is a memory that has stayed with me to this day and one that I have often thought about, wondering about all sorts of 'what ifs'. Dad Charles frequented the pub on many a Saturday night usually spending a couple of hours there, typically from 4–6 pm. This habit did not sit well with mum Annie. She also visited the pub, not for an ale but to throw coal at Charles!

Back at home, Annie would scream at me,

"Go down to the police station and tell them your father is acting threateningly," I didn't know what to do, and just stood there.

"Go on," she said, "go and tell them to come and sort your father out."

I felt torn between obeying mother and reporting on my father. It was not a thing a young lad should have to do, especially when it seemed to be more a case of Annie trying to get back at Charles rather than her trying to protect herself against the risk of violence. I don't really know why she wouldn't go down there herself. Maybe she feared approaching the police on her own?

Truth was, dad Charles enjoyed his weekly pub visit and Annie did not. I think Annie may well have experienced previous upsets in her life of a similar nature.

Down at the police station the advice was simple and straightforward,

"Young lad, please go home and look after your mother"

That was fine and I had pretty much expected the police to say as much. They did offer further explanation though, instructing me,

"You need to tell your mother not to bother the police by reporting harmless domestic arguments. If things become violent, then that is another matter. Do you understand young man?"

I understood but it still troubled me that the police thought I could sort out the problem without any help from them.

They had not finished giving me instructions either for as I was leaving, the desk sergeant advised,

"And also tell your mother that if she sends you down here to complain again, then we shall be coming to your home to sort out your parents, and sort the whole damn lot of you out."

How was I going to tell Annie about that? She was likely to think I had chickened out of visiting the police station.

Things change over time – today police responses are measured in how many minutes it takes them to check in with the complainant at the scene of the alleged crime.

Earlier on, as I have mentioned, Annie had stopped badgering me when I produced a knife and threatened her with it; now, she found herself having to stop sending her young stepson to the police station, after the police threatened to sort us all out. With the family told to sort out their own domestic disputes, Annie had little choice but to try using alternative tactics.

Mum Annie may have seemed to be a bit of a battle-axe, however she was a hard working lady who diligently spent many a waking hour looking after the extended family. She would rise at 5 am, often starting with the washing. Washes were done using an old wooden scrubbing board. Clothes were first scrubbed and put in a timeworn wooden washtub which was located underneath the house.

An old scrubbing board - great for knuckles and skin!

For hot washing the procedure involved putting the washing – clothes, sheets, towels etc into a rather large copper. The copper was made of concrete and lined on the inside with a thin copper sheet (hence called a copper). The scrubbing board would be stood up in the tub or in a large tin washing bowl placed on the floor. The washing was then scrubbed up and down and sideways for as long as it took to get it somewhere near clean. Knuckles ended up red and skin sometimes peeled away, having been softened in the wash water. To warm up the water, a fire was lit under the copper in a small grated concrete pit. One of the regular duties for my brothers and sisters was to gather wood from the neighbourhood to use to stoke the fire. Once the water heated up Annie would turn the washing over and with a large pole, and carefully transfer it all to one of two side by side tubs. One of these tubs was filled with cold water. Annie had to be careful not to scold herself while transferring the washing, as the water in the copper was boiling. Taken from the cold tub, the washing was put through the ringer. The ringer was simply a device with two rubber rollers turned with a mechanical handle. I helped willingly with the heavy loads such as blankets. Not that I was too keen on it though.

Not this one ...but something 'almost' like this one. (Source: www. Motherhood in mexico.com (discontinued site))

In the basement was the only toilet. Anyone visiting the private room was kept company by a population of creepy crawlies and rather large wetas which had set up home down there. Not surprising considering the darkish, damp conditions under the house. The wetas may have come in on the wood my younger brothers had collected in the evenings or they may have come in from neighbouring hedges.

With the washing done by 7 am there was still plenty for Annie to do throughout the rest of the day. She would make her own soap in an old kerosene tin by using melted lard and a powdered washing soda. In that mix would go a 'blue bag' – a chemical or bleach ingredient meant to wash whites whiter.

The 'blue bag' of chemicals essential for turning whites whiter. (Source: www.nma.gov.au. Photo by Kipley Nink (left) www.old & interesting. Poster designed by W H Margetson, 1910.)

Tough as it was, the usual daily tasks – such as making beds, mending clothes - all needed attention and couldn't be left for another day. Linoleum was a common floor covering in those days. Just maintaining the lino in a presentable shiny condition on its own required a lot of devotion. Annie had to wax and then polish the floors. Bee's wax was first heated and then applied with rags. Then, getting down on hands and knees the lino had to be polished with dry rags.

The Shacklock – wood or coal fired. Invented by Henry Shacklock in the late 1880s – used by many NZ households to cook food, dry clothes, heat water and to keep warm. (Source: Ian Hunter. 'Workshop industries'. Te Ara – the Encyclopaedia of New Zealand)

Cooking was one of Annie's talents. For her there was no TV to gain ideas from, no celebrity chef reality shows and no expansive food markets around the corner in which to spend time selecting from all sorts of possible ingredients. For our family, dinner was usually cooked cabbage, potatoes, leeks and corn beef. The veggies all came from dad's garden. He was so proud of that garden. No sprays or fertilisers to kill bugs or to give the garden a boost, but alternatives were found as dad used the bath water to tip over his potatoes. This helped to prevent potato blight.

Cooking done on an old range fired by burning coal meant regular maintenance was required as coal dust would clog up in the flue over time. When roaring sounds were heard in the chimney it would be a sure sign that trouble brewed. To negate the fire risk Charles would climb up his ladder outside the house, clamber onto the roof and place a damp sack over the stack to extinguish any flames finding their way up the flue. Regular chimney sweeps also helped lower the fire risk. Swept back down the flue, the black coal soot made an awful mess all over the floor in the kitchen area. Mums faced the challenge of achieving a happy balance between doing a chimney sweep every so often and risk having a sooty mess in the kitchen or leaving the soot to build up in the flue and risk fire.

Four or five well known artist's pictures decorated the kitchen walls. While our family did without treats, our parents were happy to purchase a few works of art. I think for them, it brightened up the house and maybe allowed them to dream a little. One was a Rembrandt and one a Vincent Van Gogh. I thought that these paintings were valuable and that they may have been originals. (*Surely this thinking would have been an extreme long shot!*) At the end of one gardening season father burnt the paintings in a garden fire – to get rid of the borer which had invaded the picture frames. (*Hopefully they were not originals and getting rid of the borer was justified!*).

On Saturday mornings it was time to take a senna drink – senna leaves in a cup of hot water, no sugar. Senna leaves came from a leguminous plant, a dried herb, which originated from along the Nile in Egypt and also from south and east India. The believed medicinal purpose of this drink, which was to facilitate bowel movement, was probably a good enough reason for us take it. None of us took this willingly, but we all drank it as dad Charles would stand menacingly beside the door. If the senna leaves had run out, a worse fate waited to befall us children as castor oil would have to be swallowed as an alternative. Was it just a case of mum and dad doing the right thing by us and looking after our health? I think so, since they did not appear to enjoy watching us having to drink this awful concoction.

Father Charles supported the family working for Phillips & Impey as a lead light glazier. Some of his work was fitting stained glass windows in churches. Lead was used to bind together the differently coloured and shaped glass pieces. Working with lead today is considered a significant health risk, however, it did not seem to adversely affect Charles' health. Charles contracted pneumonia in his 40s bringing him near to death. He blamed Bishop Averill, (fifth Anglican bishop of Auckland 1924–1940), for his illness. Charles believed that it was the bishop's insistence on finishing the stained glass work, no matter what the weather conditions were, that caused Charles' pneumonia. Dad lapsed into a coma during this illness. Recovery took many weeks. The local minister often came in to shave father. I recall the local doctor, Dr Rossiter, standing at the door waiting for his 30 shillings - a case of pay on demand.

After recovering from his pneumonia, Charles did not go back to glazing. He felt discouraged in not being able to return to his trade or gain full time employment. Father took on whatever jobs he could, accepting relief work if that was all that was available at the time. One job involved the menial task of plucking chickens. I don't think that was a job he was proud of but it did show his tenacity. He also worked on the development of Chamberlain Golf Course under the directions of Bob Semple, Minister of Public Works for the first Labour Government of New Zealand. A number of relief workers were given opportunities to work on this project. With bulldozers left at home or parked elsewhere, the labour intensive development involved numerous workers using basic picks and shovels to shape the fairways and continuously move rocks of all shapes and sizes.

Another skill dad possessed and put to good use was repairing the family shoes. With a sharp knife in hand he would remove what was left of the old soles and then cut new ones from strips of green rubber. The rubber was soaked in water to soften it up. To protect the soles, a steel half moon shaped cap was tacked on with brass tack nails to the heel and finally any rough edges were rasped off. Because the rubber was green, the soles were blackened with black-lead – a black dye which was also used to shine up the iron door of the family's early model Shacklock stove. A fashion consciousness existed even in those days!

Dad passed away at the age of 92, I think of natural causes since I do not recall any specific illness that dad suffered from. I was 66 and working on the Auckland wharf at the time. Dad Charles' funeral service was held at the Baptist church opposite Shaddock Street, the funeral procession then proceeded to Waikumete Cemetery where he was to be cremated. Annie, Billy, Edie, Owen and I attended but it seems Jack and Ernie did not. Why, I am not certain of.

My step mother Annie died while I was working as a painter. I remember visiting her along with Eileen, in Auckland hospital when she was ill. She and Charles were living at my step-brothers home at the time. Annie was a lady who mostly kept to herself, preferring to stay at home rather than go out visiting. She seemed reluctant to share in laughter or fun events. Annie died in the early 1950s. I do not remember her funeral.

Alma was born some two years after I was born. Alma took on the household duties after Gladys died. I always got on well with Alma; there was a fond connection there which lasted until my sister died. Alma worked for Butland Industries, a confectionery factory for some years. She married Jim Chappell, a qualified engineer. They had two children, a son, Trevor and a daughter, Pat. Pat continued to communicate with me via letter and by sending Christmas Cards. She has always done this, right up to the present time, even though her health has been deteriorating. The last Christmas card I received from her was in 2010. Eileen took on the duty of sending out our Christmas cards and one was always sent to Pat. How Pat's condition is now, I do not know. Eileen and I visited Alma every month. Alma was a very easy going person with a kind heart. Eileen got on well with her. Alma died of stomach cancer in the 1960s. Her doctor tried various remedies, encouraging her to take boiled vegetable and plant extracts. None of these seemed to offer a cure. She was the first of my brothers or sisters to pass away.

Jack, two or three years younger than me, worked with a mate in a little shop on Mt Eden road, in a business recovering Chesterfield Suites. I last saw Jack around 30 years ago after I had dropped in to see him in his shop while passing by. Eileen stayed in the car while I went in to see Jack. It appeared to me that Jack was under the influence (not an uncommon thing) and so the visit was short. Jack moved to Whitianga about 10 years ago and he passed away there at the age of 93 in August 2011, the same week as Eileen passed away. I received a phone call from Whitianga informing me of Jack's passing while at the same time I was grieving for Eileen. I had always got on well with Jack and would have liked to see him more often. This did not happen.

Irene was my second sister and she worked in a laundry washing business. I felt that Alma and her younger sister never really got on with each other and witnessed on occasion how they fought and argued. Irene received a few setbacks in her life including a work accident when she amputated three fingers after trapping them in a ringer. Irene visited me on the Auckland wharfs, suddenly appearing one day and asking me if she could stay with me and Eileen. It seems Irene was crying out for help. Eileen was not so keen on this idea considering Irene a troublesome character. I wonder how Irene felt about this 'rejection' but I don't really know nor do I know the reasons why she wanted to stay with the family. Irene responded by complaining to Social Welfare about not being taken in. Most likely this would have been as a result of her feeling rejected rather than because of a vindictive grudge she had. Sadly, some five years later Irene passed away suffering from breast cancer. I did not attend the funeral as I wasn't made aware of Irene's passing. Thinking of how all this could have been different is a reoccurring thought that has remained with me as I reflect on things gone by. I have experienced pangs of regret from time to time. Not visiting Irene in Mt Eden while she was suffering from cancer was another regret and a situation I wish I had handled differently. Torn between wanting to visit and Eileen's reluctance not to, was like being stuck between a rock and a hard place and tore at my heartstrings.

Irene had married a Samoan gentleman some 20 years her senior. A noticeable characteristic of his were his false teeth which always seemed to be close to falling out when he spoke or laughed. Irene passed away some two years after her husband did.

Ernie was the last born. For a while, he with I both worked on the same Matamata farm, however he was later employed mainly as a shoe repairer fixing school children's and working people's shoes. This occupation supported him quite well. Having observed dad repairing the family shoes stood Ernie in good stead and helped him to eventually set up his own small business. Ernie and I got on well, as I did with Alma and Jack. Ernie was the only sibling I told about my intentions of leaving home after my having had an argument with father Charles. Ernie went to Fiji during the war; however he did not see any active service there as his posting was mainly targeted as a training exercise. Ernie married Joyce Woolley and they had two children, Dennis and Maureen. When Ernie lived in Dominion Road prior to moving to Army Bay, he and Joyce befriended an elderly chap and often paid him visits and shared cups of tea. When the old man died Ernie visited the house and somehow ended up with his half-crown collection. Some mystery there!

Ernie and Joyce moved to Army Bay. Although I got on okay with Ernie and Joyce, visiting was none too frequent. There was a bit of 'we'll visit you if you visit us first' but visiting didn't happen. I recall once meeting Ernie outside Orewa New World, Ernie smoking outside while Joyce shopped inside. We had a small chat and that was it, we didn't invite each other over for a cup of tea or anything. It just didn't happen.

Joyce's mother and father often visited Con and Nan Evans on Sundays for scones and tea. They were related to each other in some way. It was Joyce who had urged me to call Eileen and ask her for a date after we met at the Crystal Palace. You might think that this would endear Joyce to Eileen, but it did not. For some reason the two argued off and on. Eileen did not like Joyce. I never really got to know the reason for this long standing grudge. No doubt this state of affairs had some bearing on why visits were so infrequent. It was difficult to make mention of Joyce to Eileen, as I felt that any reference to Joyce would just antagonise Eileen. And so I remained quiet to keep the peace.

Ernie and Joyce played bowls at the Silverdale Bowling Club. Although close in proximity to the Orewa Bowling Club we only once played in the same tournament. Eileen enjoyed the competitive side of bowling and she quietly mentioned to me one day that she would have liked to have played Joyce and Ernie and to have beaten them.

Both Ernie and his wife Joyce enjoyed a smoking habit. At around 80 or so Joyce died of emphysema even though she had given the cigarettes away for some five years. Ernie grieved heavily for Joyce. His son, Dennis, told his father to return to Australia with daughter Maureen who had come over for the funeral. This he did, staying with Maureen for approximately four years. Ernie never settled down and continued to pine for Joyce, making life difficult for Maureen who had a boyfriend at the time. Looking after Ernie was becoming too much for her and it was inevitable that he would have to enter a rest home, be he ready to or not. Ernie never really got over losing Joyce and he passed away in Australia in 2009 at about 90. At that time I received a call from Dennis advising Ernie had died. This was unexpected and shocked me. Again I could not attend the funeral. Dennis Knill apparently became a successful business man in the travel industry, mainly through generating travel blog stories which he sold to the press. Joyce told Eileen about Dennis' success but it wasn't believed.

Billy Beesley was my stepbrother. Billy, like Jack, worked as an upholsterer. Billy married Edie and they initially lived at Shaddock Street for some four years. While I got on with Edie, step-mum Annie and later Eileen harboured suspicions that I had eyes for Edie

– rivers do not always run smooth. Annie threatened to tell Billy about this while Billy was in the islands.

Billy went to Green Island (part of the Pacific Islands) having been conscripted into the army (I was a volunteer). Billy wrote back describing the 'action' he saw over there. He was attached to the New Zealand 3rd Division – the main fighting formation of the 2nd N.Z.E.F. (I.P.). However, although the 3rd Division never fought as a formation, its component brigades became involved in semi-independent actions as part of the Allied forces in the Solomon Islands, Treasury Islands and Green Island. He talked about fighting the Japanese but I felt his talk may have exaggerated his role.

Billy also travelled to Fiji, usually returning with American cigarettes and selling them in New Zealand thereby establishing a little side business for himself. On his return he went to work on the Auckland wharfs. In his later years he lived in Red Beach. He passed away in the late 1990s. I had met Billy a few times around the Orewa shops but I was not aware of when he passed away.

Owen Beesley was my second stepbrother. It was easier to get on with Owen than it was with Billy. Owen commented that Billy was a skite and that he didn't like his brother. Owen worked as a builder's labourer and then as a shoe repairer. He was not an academic person but was a kind hearted soul. He married a Samoan lady. I can only remember them making a single visit to us in Florence Avenue.

Contact with Owen was lost after that and it seemed that he had just disappeared. It is uncertain as to what eventuated in Owens life. He apparently lived in Auckland but I know nothing of his later years.

Having four brothers and two sisters, I always had family around me. Contact with my siblings was limited through the years, especially after we had all left home. Apart from Pat (Patricia-Alma and Jim Chapel's daughter) in Australia sending Christmas cards, the only sort of regular contact we had was with Jack who sent Christmas cards and longish letters from Whitianga. In these he talked about fishing and retirement. I would write back. Jack must have developed his love of fishing after leaving home, because our father Charles, really only ever took me out fishing as the other siblings did not seem so interested.

An important part in anyone's family life involves the relationships they develop and surround themselves with, between parents and siblings and between the siblings themselves. Over the years Pop regrettably lost touch with most of his family. This manifests itself in different ways throughout Pop's story. A case in point is seen when Pop was informed that his brother Jack had died in Whitianga in the very week that Pop's Eileen passed away in North Shore hospital in August 2011. Jack's passing saddened Pop. He expressed it as a 'double whammy'. Many times since in reminiscing about life a regret or two surfaces, one being of how important it is to maintain contact and not lose it. People seem to just disappear once regular contact is lost. Only by having maintained contact could Pop have better understood how events shaped the lives and attitudes of his family members. This wasn't appreciated until much later and by then it was much too late. Example – Irene's troubles were more than likely a cry for help. There were few visits but many a thought of 'I wonder what happened to?'

For whatever reason, he attended very few of his families' funerals, it just didn't seem to happen.

CHAPTER 2

CHILDHOOD YEARS

SHADDOCK STREET, MT EDEN

Second Home – Shaddock Street

In 1920 our family moved to Shaddock Street in Mt Eden. I was four years old and almost ready to attend my first school - Grafton Primary.

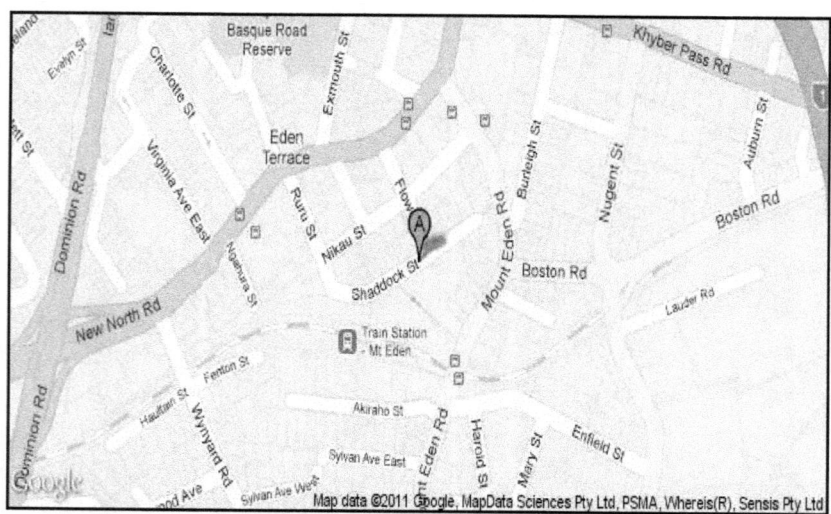

Map shows Shaddock Street, in Mount Eden. (Source: Google Maps)

Growing up in a family of seven and losing mum when I was only eight years old made life a bumpy road to travel. I envied people lucky enough to have real mothers to bring them up. Dad Charles had promised the children that he would keep the family together. When I left home at 14, Charles was upset at my leaving, and for me this was something I have regretted ever since, more so as time has gone on. My stepmother Annie had to mother seven children, which could never have been easy. I don't think I ever really knew much about the events that shaped her life.

Mt Eden – 1950 (Source: Sir George Grey Special Collections, Auckland Libraries, 7-A10930)

Certain life events while they may seem insignificant to many outside of the family are in turn remembered with degrees of regret and involve unresolved questions by those living within the family. This was so for Pop. A simple example of this is what Pop remembers as the bread allocation rations, where Billy and Owen always got two slices of bread with jam, and Pop only ever got single slices. This perceived (or otherwise) favouritism had big impacts on Pop and seemed to influence aspects of his life. Whether any justification existed for his responses or how dramatic the reality was, we may not get to know. It seemed to be a factor in his decision to leave home a short time after having an argument with his father over Billy seeming to get preferred treatment. The death of his birth mother, Gladys, could also have troubled him more than he realised.

Another childhood memory of mine related to my so called naughtiness at about six years of age when my punishment from Gladys would consist of whacks across my backside with a brush. I suppose most of us remember similar sorts of things but for me, my mother's response seemed a fairly dramatic reaction to what I thought were mostly innocuous misdemeanours.

After Gladys passed away my father, Charles, would visit the local pub on most Saturday nights, something that stepmother Annie was not too happy about. She was none too keen on being left alone in the evenings.

Shaddock Street, Mt Eden, 1931- in there at the back somewhere! (Source: Sir George Grey Special Collections, Auckland Libraries, 4-5174)

Our Shaddock Street home was located close to the city. When my brothers were about 10 -12 years old and on occasions as bored as I was, we would sometimes occupy ourselves by wandering around Symonds Street taking in the business of the shops and as the urge grabbed us, sight unseen, we would nick a few bananas or pineapple tins. Naughty lads we were! Accomplices in crime were some of the Turnock children who we played with from time to time. The Turnocks were a large family of 11. They lived down at the bottom end of Shaddock Street.

Family dinner table sittings offer many memories for many a family. Dad Charles would sit at the head of the table, stick lying in easy reach of his hand. With all five children (later seven) seated at the table it was difficult for us to sit there without opening our mouths to speak. Charles insisted dinner was for eating and not for chatting. Chit-chat was for after dinner. While my father did have rules and stuck to them, we didn't see him as overly authoritarian but more as someone who strived to be happy. In those days, be it in the classroom, at home or in the police station, 'light' physical discipline was not frowned upon and was more or less considered as a common practice – 'spare the rod and spoil the child'.

I walked this road – only a few streets across from Shaddock St. (Source - Sir George Grey Special Collections, Auckland Libraries, 35-R190)

Games Children Play

Whatever the hassles at home might be, children will naturally go out and discover fun for themselves. For my brothers and me, fun was riding down steep slopes on sleds. For anyone who knows the geography of Auckland, it is easy to imagine finding a hilly slope when you are in possession of a sled. There were plenty of slopes in and around Mt Eden and then there was the Mt Eden hill itself. There were always the bully boys too, who would be on the prowl to steal and then runaway with our sleds, too lazy to, or not knowing how to build their own.

Our sleds were homemade. We built them from wood taken from discard bins at a local car manufacturer's yard. In the automobile business, the wood, a type of sapwood, was fitted to the car's roof profile, over which was fitted a tight black canvas type material. No such extras on today's cars! One of the cars utilising this design was the Ford T, a popular model of the time, although there weren't too many models to choose from. What also made this wood particularly suitable for sleds was the slight curvature at one end, where the wood was formed to fit the curve of the car's roof design. Naturally we would always ask for permission to be allowed to take the discarded wood, however, if no one was attending the yard, what would kids desperate to slide down hillsides do? We went and 'borrowed' the wood. Naughty we were! The sleds were made with two wooden strips on either side bridged with a piece of wood acting as the seat. The steeper the hill the faster the sleds travelled. To stop we simply tipped out the side, voluntarily or involuntarily. Interestingly the only thing that really got hurt was sometimes a bit of pride when we failed to complete the course. In all of the hundreds of sled slides we did, we never suffered an injury involving more than a little skin being removed.

I wonder how 'Politically Correct' things were in those days. No Department of Labour inspectors either I think. Taking risks appeared to be an 'occupational hazard'.

Another enjoyment of ours was skating at the Khyber Pass rink. Once again we Knills didn't kill ourselves and all of us must have been well balanced as the worst accidents resulted in just a few skinned knees. It was a case of bring your own skates. Our skates were not of a fancy design, being of a simple adjustable sliding middle section – one size fits all. Loosen the nut, slide to fit, retighten, strap in and skate.

The Deluxe Roller Skating Rink
(Source: Auckland Council – Libraries – Heritage Images – 7-A1615)

For entertainment options not requiring us to buy equipment or pay an entry fee, there was the Gribblehurst Park swamp with its frogs and tadpoles, little creatures waiting to be placed into our glass jars. Once captured, we took the amphibians home and transferred them to larger bowls, and then proudly placed the bowls onto the lounge mantelpiece for display and observation. Wasn't every child of the time expected to learn about the metamorphosis of tadpoles into frogs?

When the Australian Wirth's Bros Circus Ltd came to town, locating itself on land next to the railway sheds at Parnell, our family would take a walk down to the waterfront to see the big top with its circus animals. There were elephants, tigers, lions and horses along with the predictable clowns. Next door stood Lunar Fun Park with its roller coaster, Ferris wheel rides and side shows. How we longed to get onto them. We were not a rich family.

Pedal bikes have been a favourite with me all of my life. I rode them as a lad and still ride them today in 2011. Only last month, I took a journey up to the Orewa shops on my trusty bike, the mudguards protecting my tracksuit pants from splashes of mud. I rode up the road minus my helmet which I had left at home in the garage and I wasn't about to go back and get it. I got to the roundabout up the road where the local constable stopped me and asked,

"Why sir, did you let cars wait for you while you crossed the roundabout?"

I calmly explained to the officer, "Sir, I woke up this morning with a bad headache, I could not manage to get my breakfast down." Seeing that he needed a little more convincing, I felt I needed to add a little more detail,

"I know I wasn't wearing my helmet officer, I couldn't as it would have aggravated my condition"

"I'd rather you walk than take your bicycle next time."

The officer then left without saying any more. I presumed he left letting me make up my own mind about carrying on or returning home.

I think that the constable must have been impressed – surely!

Monarch bikes. My father purchased a Monarch like this for me from Farmers in Hobson Street.

Much earlier on, at the other end of my life, there was the monthly bike ride I took riding over metal roads from Mt Eden all the way to Helensville. Each month, Ernie and I would meet up with one or two neighbourhood kids and off we would go. The 37 mile (59 kilometres) journey was accomplished in a few hours. My bike – a Monarch, may have been fancy at the time but it didn't really compare to the carbon fibre, 23 speed models of today. I was not lucky enough to own any 'Speedo's' or clip-on bike shoes. The tyres on my bike were thick and solid and must have done the job as I can't recall ever having had a puncture. My dear father purchased this lovely machine for me from Farmers in Hobson Street. Needless to say the hot pools at Helensville were a slice of heaven! The journey back not so!

Father Charles took me along to soccer matches at Blanford Park in the city. We would walk up Wellesley Street to Queen Street and on to Anzac Ave to the football ground located in a gully. Dad was a side line supporter as so many parents are, often standing in deep mud shouting encouragement at me, especially when I had the ball and the goalmouth beckoned.

I think my love of fishing may well have developed from dad taking me on walks from Mt Eden, down Khyber Pass to the Parnell Baths over bridge and along the walkway to the waterfront where the fish were meant to be hanging around. Not too many were waiting there for us however as stingray were the only fish eager enough to come and have a look at what was on our hooks. Maybe it was the green cord line we used as a substitute for nylon which scared the real fish off. When a stingray was caught (dad always used trevally bait) the flaps were cut off and taken home to be cooked. The whole family partook of stingray fried in dripping which we ate with bread. There were no bones and having to deal with the odd bit of gristle just added to the mix. The love of fishing stayed with me all my life. In retirement I was lucky enough to be able to enjoy fishing with my next door neighbour, Neville.

Family Outings

While our family found life tough living in the depression years, dad Charles and Annie took us on weekend trips to Beachlands whenever they could. Step mum Annie would take pots, cabbages, beans and potatoes and a steel grate from home. Pine trees stood where now tar sealed roads sit and lifestyle homes have replaced wild patches of weeds and trees. Gathering small pine branches and a few pinecones we lit a small fire and cooked the food. Maybe healthy, but a feed not exactly looked forward to by us children. Dad loved to bring out his Model A for the weekend drive. The car was father's pride and joy. Always polished, especially after rain, it sat proud in the car park at Beachlands.

Saturday night Speedway at Western Springs entertained us all. Remembered are the concrete seats, hard on our bums without cushions to sit on, and the penny ice creams we never refused. Only the motorbikes raced in the 1920s, there weren't any speed cars racing. The noise generated by the bikes got us all excited. The area where the speedway was located had previously been a waste land contaminated by council abattoirs, tallow works, tanneries and fell mongers. These businesses used to dump their waste in streams at Motions Creek.

Speedway rise set for big night in front of the crowd at Western Springs. (Source: Gordon McIsaac, www.speedwayclub.co.nz)

Town Hall wrestling featuring Lofty Blomfield provided another form of amusement which we enjoyed going to. Father commented that matches were 'fixed', however he still took us there. Who said things change? Once in a while 'guest' wrestlers would top the bill. One of these promotions included an American troupe featuring the 'Man Mountain'. Cheering, loud cheering reverberated around the arena whenever the 'Mountain' seemed to be caught in an inescapable hold. Part of the fun was figuring out if the matches were fixed or not.

The annual Easter Show held at the nearby Epsom Show grounds was enjoyed for the sideshows we tried to win something at, and for the candyfloss offered there. Competitors at the wood chopping competitions were cheered on by enthusiastic audiences and by us. We brought the family billy along to the show to fill it with free milk offered at the completion of milking exhibitions. Being as resourceful as we were, we knew how to make the most of any 'offers' going. You might say 'we milked it'

Bullies

Bully boys hung around the streets and town centres as they do today. My brother Ernie was troubled by one particular bully who applied his trade to my baby brother. It was Ernie's job most evenings to collect firewood from around the neighbourhood to fuel our stove and copper washer. Off he would go in the direction of the domain with his trusty steel-wheeled trolley This particular little scoundrel, obviously aware of Ernie's movements, saw the youngest Knill as an easy target. Whether he was after firewood without having to go and collect it himself, I don't know. I soon picked up that there may have been a problem after Ernie had confided in me,

"Charlie, there's a rather nasty chap who waits for me to go collecting firewood and then comes and annoys me. What should I do?"

I thought about it a bit and then that evening I suggested to Ernie, "Look, you march along as usual and I shall follow up about 100 yards behind. And don't run away."

Sure enough the predictable happened and the bully once again accosted Ernie. I approached from out of the blue and the bully took off fast with me in pursuit. However he was no match for my superior speed and after catching him I gave him something to remember, telling him in no uncertain terms,

"Try that again and next time I'll break both your arms."

This particular bully never approached Ernie again. Case closed!

School

The early school years for us five Knill and later with the two Beasley boys were spent attending Grafton Primary School. Every morning we would take the 20 minute walk down Mt Eden Road to Nugent Street and on to school. Not too many exciting things happened at Grafton School other than an occasion when two giant oaks came crashing down during a storm. I remember the wide asphalt playgrounds, as asphalt had only just come into vogue and was a rather new phenomenon during those days. However it was the fact that our lunches often went missing (stolen) that prompted Annie to rescue us from what had become to mum a wayward school. Thus Annie went looking for a more 'respectable' school. The one she chose for us was to be a school with 'religion'. After a few enquires were made, St Benedict's which happened to be nearby, was selected. I felt very comfortable here and managed quite well. Over time I gained fond memories of Sister Bertle. She was the headmistress who treated me fairly but with strictness as teaches should (I think most nuns were like that in those days?). The fact that I got on so well there endowed me with the privilege of being appointed chief convent lawn mower. What has stayed with me over the years are fond memories of those brown garmented nuns who always kept a watchful and caring eye over the children they cared for and I was one of them.

After finishing school at St Benedict's I moved on to the Marist Brothers at Vermont Street, so continuing the 'religious' element.

Was there a religious conviction behind moving the boys on to religious schools? Or was it more a security aspect, maybe where less harm could afford the boys and where lunches were kept safe? Whatever the reason for the change it must have been done with a caring intent.

Vermont Street School – 1920s. (Source: Marist Brothers.org.nz/about us/province-beginnings/buildings)

Brother Calixtus was the boss at Vermont Street. Brother was a 'hard' man, a man who loved sport. A typical sporting event was the class run around the neighbourhood block. My thin build seemed to be ideally suited to such an exercise as I must have resembled an ultra distance marathon runner. I never needed conditioning to be that way, and I have been so proportioned all my life. Involvement in sport was a big thing at school and I was expected (compelled you might say) to be part of it. Rugby in the winter and cricket in the summer was the staple diet as other sports struggled to get a look in. Sixpence was charged as a contribution towards the gear. Never destined to become a celebrity sportsman I nevertheless enjoyed it all.

The different character of private Catholic schools manifests itself in different ways. Most of us who have attended such schools will have stories to tell and memories of brother so and so or sister so and so. They brought a dimension not always seen in state schools. This must have had something to do with a collective religious belief and a giving of self for those beliefs. There have been times when institutional problems impacted negatively on some student's lives but in the most part life at school was tough, strict but fair. School life was a positive preparation for entering into the outside world. Pop felt that life would have been harder had he not experienced this religious element. There was a caring nature present in most brothers and sisters he came across and he recognised this.

On one occasion as I recall, a certain Irish priest came out to school to give lessons. In our class down the back of the room, a certain adventurous lad thought that chatting during class was the thing to do. Needless to say the priest was well aware of such shenanigans and suddenly appeared at the back of the room next to the lad and proceeded to hand out a very crisp slap across the head.

"Behave yourself young man, do not chatter in my class" was all he said.

Class masters would not be allowed to get away with that today!

Considering that my brothers and I were 'transferred' to a Marist school, it was not surprising to me that eventually we would be 'encouraged' to join the Catholic faith. Annie was already aware of this and she told me it was something you had to do at a church school. And so it wasn't long before I started preparing for my First Confession and First Holy Communion. White shirts, red sashes, rosary beads and a catechism became part of the formality in making my preparations. These religious experiences had an effect on the belief systems I ended up with. Years later when I was a young soldier I experienced a feeling of being spared to fight another day whilst under fire amongst the olive trees of Greece and again a similar feeling of being saved when not being seen by German fighters while exposed on the cargo deck sailing from Greece to Egypt. In reflecting on these incidents, my feelings alternate between putting it all down to luck or those of a guiding hand from above being present and setting me for other things.

School was school and work was work in 1930. Those in the lower economic classes often entered the workforce after Standard 6 and there would be no exception for me. University was beyond many, and it was for us. Dad Charles expected an early entry into work. These were the years of the Great Depression.

The Great Depression Years in New Zealand, Late 1920s – 1935

This story cannot be told without some background to a particular time in New Zealand history when life was as tough as it ever could have been – the depression years of the late 1920s through to 1935, at its worst between 1931 and 1932. Appreciating the circumstances throws some light on what Pop and his family must have experienced through this time. With five siblings, their birth mum having passed away, and now with two step brothers, the looming depression meant further education was out of the question. Just to find a job and thus be able to support the family was a blessing. Many children were deprived of any education beyond school leaving age. They were compelled to leave school and take any work, at however small a wage just to help the family survive. For most New Zealanders this was a time of enormous stress, hunger and despair.

The depression saw incomes fall by 40%, exports fall by 45%, wool values decline by 60% and farm incomes dip below zero. Many farmers walked off their land unable to keep up with mortgage payments. Unemployment peaked (estimated at up to 100,000) especially in the North Island. In 1930 there were no dole payments for the unemployed to rely on. Relief work was offered, mainly consisting of working on the roads. Church and community organisations set up 'soup kitchens' for the hungry. In Auckland, in April of 1932, unemployed men fought police in two nights of rioting. Pop knew what 'soup kitchens' were all about and while not a regular visitor he did visit for an occasional 'top up'

With the conditions easing by 1935 a new Labour Party came into power. The Party established the first Welfare state introducing free healthcare, free education, assistance for the elderly and infirm and unemployment assistance.
(Source – www.nzhistory.net.nz/culture/1920s/overview)

Pull together Depression cartoon, 1933 (Source:
http://www.nzhistory.net.nz/media/photo/pull-together-depression-cartoon
Ministry for Culture and Heritage, updated 29 March 2012)

Road making during the Depression, by unknown photographer, 1932. (Source: Alexander Turnbull Library. 1/2-022602-F)

It was in this climate that we struggled on as a family and having to leave school early was something we had to accept. The need to work and contribute to the family income over ruled any thought of going on to achieve a higher education.

CHAPTER 3

THE KNILL FAMILY –

MY WORKING LIFE BEGINS

With the depression having set in and with no end in sight, all my family siblings, including myself, were encouraged to go out into the world and earn a few shillings to support the family finances. School ended for me at Standard 6 and so into the wide world of work I was thrust.

In my first job at a mere 13 or 14 years of age, I earned a grand total of five shillings. These hard earned wages were handed over to my step mum Annie, who would return sixpence to me. You could purchase a pound of bananas for a penny. Carrots were the same – a penny for a pound. Milk was four pence and a hot pie four pence.

The Auckland morning newspaper, the *New Zealand Herald*, was a favourite place to look for work, there not being many other options. I saw a job advertised at Abbott, Armstrong and Howie, men and women's hat makers and I duly applied. The acceptance letter came in the mail, and so off I went to join the labour force. The firm was located on Albert Street off a small side road. The Shamrock Hotel stood on the corner of the street. My first job involved transporting finished hats in a wicker basket to a warehouse located a little down the road. No forklifts or couriers in these days. Hats were made on large moulding machines cooled with water systems. Hat styles were moulded on specially designed rubber moulds. Felt was placed on the moulds and buttons pushed to bring down the top of the machine over the mould. Steam helped shape and form the hat style.

There was no chance of learning the trade or being given an apprenticeship. I had to be satisfied with the menial manual tasks I was given.

While I liked the job, I found it difficult connecting with the boss, who frowned upon me talking with a lovely young American lady working downstairs. There would have been no complaints from me if my association with her had blossomed, but alas it did not. However I was rewarded by partaking in a free meal at the restaurant owned by the young ladies father.

The wicker baskets had four wheels fitted to their bases and each basket carried 20 to 30 hats. At the warehouse I would move the basket onto a lift platform, and then via a mechanical rope and pulley system I would pull the lift up to the floor level above. No electric lifts to make things easier for me.

Back at home on Sundays, Annie would cook up two dozen pies which were to be the family's lunches for the whole week. The pies tasted ok on Monday and maybe Tuesday but by Friday they had developed a rather 'musty' aroma and had become rather hard. When I lifted the crust off the top I would sometimes see blue mould decorating the edges. Still, we all ate the pies. I warmed mine up on the work boiler which provided a ready-made oven.

Choosing what footwear to wear to work just wasn't an option since I had none. The choice for me was obvious and off to work I would trudge – barefoot! After a little while earning wages Charles gave me a pair of sandshoes and then later a pair of leather shoes. These were possessions I absolutely treasured.

My father wanted to have the whole family out working as staying at school or attending university was an option he wasn't going to consider. The majority of any wages I earned working would go into the combined family pool. The extra contribution to the family income helped keep our heads above water. Our family survived.

An invitation offered to me by a Mr Hollis, a fellow worker of mine at Abbots, to attend his church is vividly remembered. Not only because it was my first 'religious' experience outside of my schooling but I would think about this experience again fighting in Greece - experiencing an angel over me when escaping death amongst the olive trees. I accepted the invitation from Mr Hollis and went with him to attend the Church of Christ in Newton, situated off Karangahape Road near Pitt Street. Of course, there was the added enticement of buns and tea on offer. That swung the deal for me. It was a common part of the service for a request to be made from the pulpit for those who wanted to publicly accept Jesus Christ to gather up the front of the church. An urge to do this saw me accepting the invitation. After that I went a few more times.

While experiencing some pressure to 'join up,' I was also feeling degrees of being 'guided' to go this way. That step never eventuated as I held back, some of my questions remaining unanswered either from the church or from myself. Many of these questions I continue to ask today. While I gave no final commitment to the church, some generous soul, a church member, gifted me a lovely heavy duty woollen overcoat. The coat was worn over many a winter. I valued that coat. Somehow the coat waited for me until I returned from overseas service. Dad Charles wondered how I had come about such a quality garment and he harboured a suspicion or two that it could have been stolen. As for the church story, Charles did not appear to believe that either.

The hat factory job lasted for three years. I realised after a little while that I was not going to become a hat 'blocker' (those who made hats). So with the likelihood of remaining at the bottom of the rack and just a message boy for the rest of my life, I began contemplating a move on to greener pastures. In the depression years the expectation was that if you were lucky enough to have a job then you should do everything to keep it, but I wouldn't let that influence any decisions I might make about changing jobs. If I felt I had enough of any particular job I would not have a problem in saying goodbye to it.

Meanwhile, my sisters and brothers were all working, fortunate indeed considering the high unemployment rates in New Zealand during the depression.

My sister Irene worked in a commercial bag washing business. The laundry company was owned by a foreign gentleman, possibly a Czechoslovakian man. The owner ran the business under a tight rein. Local area businesses sent large cloth bags containing items such as towels, aprons, overalls and hospital gear to be washed. It was Irene's job to process materials by guiding them through large hot rollers. These rollers were two metres or so wide and used steam in the pressing operation. It was while working on this process that Irene got some of her fingers trapped and had to have three of them amputated. She tried to get reparation, however without accident compensation; the only remedy was to sue the business owner. In those times that was easier said than done. Dad Charles sought compensation from the Compensation Court, from which Irene received only a token amount. Left with three stumps on her hand where her fingers had been, Irene found it difficult to get back to any normality. In reflecting on this, and considering some of Irene's later behaviour, it is quite likely that this incident robbed her of much of her independence and feelings of self worth. I felt that a struggling Irene started to send out cries for help from this point on.

Sister Alma worked at Butland Industries making confectionery. She looked after a chocolate dipping process. A favourite confectionery in the 1940s was Sonny Jims – a marshmallow, peanut and chocolate bar. A forerunner to today's Moro or Mars bars maybe? Thick cheese slices were added to the product line in later years. A dutiful servant of the company she worked there for 10 to 15 years.

Having three earners contributing to family finances certainly helped. Alma contributed around seven shillings, Irene five or six shillings and I about five. These incomes were added to the £3 Charles earned. Jack and Ernie had not yet entered the workforce. They contributed later. Ernie left school at Standard 6 and Jack a little later.

Growing tired of work at the hat factory I once again started looking in the *New Zealand Herald* job vacancies. Anyway, working for a cantankerous old boss was testing my patience thin. It irked me being told off for talking to the girls on the first floor, particularly the American lady I had eyes for. Talking to girls when you should be working was seen as a definite no-no and not permitted at all. Employed as millinery girls, they dressed hats up with ribbons and imitation flowers. In the 1930s gentlemen wore rimmed felt hats and ladies wore whatever the hat fashion dictated at the time.

As much as you may have wanted to, you didn't just jump from one job to another. The depression years were tough. Families struggled to survive. Beggars could not be choosers. Soup kitchens cropped up here and there, feeding hungry people. While I certainly did not visit soup kitchens every day, I did not have any inhibitions about visiting every now and then. In a way it helped me to gain some independence and the food served here was usually a welcome variation to the predictable dinners served at home. It was easier to look for a job with something in your stomach but I couldn't find anything at all in the city. I had to look elsewhere and it was to the country that I went looking.

Combing the vacancies in the *Herald*, I noticed a farm job advertised in Otorohanga. Why was I looking in the *Herald*? Coupled with my dissatisfaction at the hat factory I wasn't exactly thrilled with home life either. Sitting around the family dinner table one evening, dad and I got into a bit of an argument, certainly not the first one.

"You don't spend time with me anyway, I may as well leave home," I threw at him.

After a few more short exchanges I repeated my challenge.

"You wouldn't have the guts to leave home," father retorted.

"I'm not so sure."

It was a stupid argument but we had egged each other on, probably too far. For the next few days I stewed on how we had threatened each other. Enough had been said for me to make up my mind that if a suitable job came up I would leave home.

Ernie quizzed me, asking why I seemed agitated.

"Ernie, I've decided to leave home and go and look for a job out on a farm somewhere."

"Why would you want to do that?" he asked me.

I didn't see the need to explain any further and said no more. Ernie happened to be the only one I told of these intentions.

At the time I was only a lad of 13. There were no labour rules governing minimum working age. My decision to leave home had been made. The way I went about it however, is something I have regretted ever since. I don't think my father or I really wanted the leaving to happen, evidenced by certain behaviours on both our parts later on, however we threw challenges at each other which seemed to create a situation where neither of us felt we could back down from.

After accepting the advertised job, off I went by train to work for the Cowley family in Otorohanga. There were three Cowley brothers, Mark, Thead and Tom, each owning a farm. I worked on Tom

Cowley's farm. The work here was enjoyable and the family looked after me. It was certainly different to working in the enclosed confines of a hat factory. There was a variety of work such as roping calves' legs, washing cows' udders, making silage. The farm carried a herd of about 45 cows and three farm dogs. Milking was done by Tom but part of my job was to round up the cows and herd them into one of three milking stalls (called the shed). These would have looked something like horse racing starting stalls. Once each cow was milked, a rod was pulled and the cow exited. It was onto the next stall, and so the process repeated. Milking was twice a day. The idea was to 'strip' cows dry as leaving milk in the udders risked causing udder disease.

Cow dung was used to fertilise paddocks. Dung would be collected and piled up around the milking shed, then when needed it would be picked up and loaded onto a type of trailer sled and taken by horse to be spread out across the farm's paddocks. Not a very clean job!

Hugh Stringleman and Frank Scrimgeour
(Source : Alexander Turnbull Library - Hugh Stringleman and Frank Scrimgeour. 'Dairying and dairy products', Te Ara - the Encyclopaedia of New Zealand - www.TeAra.govt.nz/en/dairying-and-dairy-products/4/2)

Milk went into separators with the separated cream going into two large steel cans. The remaining (watered) milk would be used as calf feed. The steel cans were taken to the road, to await pick up by private transporters to be in turn taken to the local dairy company located in Te Awamutu. Contents were weighed and quality assessed after which official payment advice notes were left in the empty cans ready to be returned to the farm.

A particular enjoyment for me was going down to the back of the farm with a .22 rifle and shooting rabbits. The dead rabbits were given to the farm dogs. Along the back of the farm ran the Waipa River. Fencing needed continual attention especially near river areas. We made fence posts and battens from straight pieces of felled willow trees. A good selection of willow trees was available to choose from. Once a tree was chosen, we felled it with an axe and hand saws and then cut the tree into batten-sized lengths. The trunk cuts were split into battens and trimmed with the saws.

Tom Cowley donned a black suit every month and would be off to the local Masonic Lodge. Wives did not go. While the Cowleys looked after me much like one of their own, it was the Cowleys adopted son who began to cause problems for me. A bit of a brat, he liked to play tricks on me by putting a bucket of water above the door and have it tip over my head as I entered the room. This annoyed me no end and after having worked on the farm for one or two years and still wondering sometimes if I might be better off at home, I started contemplating a move away from Otorohanga.

Onwards and upwards I thought and soon another farm job came along working for Gathern Wright in Matamata. Again there was leg roping to be done and washing udders. Unlike the Cowley farm, here there were no milking machines and so milking was done by hand into a bucket. Again cows had to be stripped, i.e. milked out. This farm had approximately 35 cows in the herd. Three of us did the milking (by hand) in an eight bale outside shed.

Cream was separated from the milk. Buckets filled with milk were tipped into stainless steel separators. Separation was started by manually cranking the separator for a few minutes, and then switching to an electrical system which quickly took over. Calves were reared for a short time and then put out at the farm gate. These sold at the princely sum of one shilling (hence the name 'bobby calves'). Accommodation was a little hut sort of building – a bed along with a curtain closed wardrobe and not much else.

For night time entertainment I purchased my first crystal set at an electrical shop in Matamata. Radios were to always be a close companion of mine throughout my life. Out at the farm listening to 'radio talk' kept me in touch with city folk. At night, I tuned into 3ZM, entertained in my own little world. It was pretty much 3ZM or 1YA, as options were limited and certainly no 'pirate' radio stations broadcast in the 1930s. The cows stood calmly, pacified during milking by music, fed to them through a loudspeaker hooked up in the shed, fed by a 100 metres or so aerial line run to the shed from the farmhouse. In later years my radio would be tuned in for early Saturday morning 'scratchings' and afternoon races and then for talkback radio especially as bedside companions in retirement years.

Dinner time announcements at the farm came from the homestead's porch, meals served on an enamel plate, collected at the porch and taken back to the hut to be eaten. Working arrangements here were strictly one of boss and farm hand. Life was devoid of any meaningful social interactions.

Typical milking process – 1930s (Source: www.pukeariki.com/research /taranaki research centre/taranaki stories. PHO2006-281)

While working on the farm, I mentioned to the boss that my brother Ernie was looking for work. The Wrights soon offered Ernie a position. However I harboured suspicions that once Ernie started, the Wrights may well let me go in favour of Ernie. What didn't help was getting yelled at for tipping over a half filled bucket of milk while doing the milking. These verbal admonishments I took to heart and worried about. It did me no good.

Such incidents seemed rather minor in nature to me but not to my boss it appears, and so didn't make for a happy work environment at all. Work here certainly ended up being less enjoyable than working for Tom Cowley. Lightening never strikes twice they say but for me it did and I again found myself being bullied by one of the family sons. I gradually became dissatisfied with farm life at Matamata and felt increasingly uncomfortable here. However it was the fact that three of the Wright's cows got the "staggers" and the resulting financial difficulties for the farm that may have finally tipped the balance. The poor financial situation resulted in both Ernie and me being asked to leave the farm. It was the end of a short six months or so spent at Matamata.

Deciding to stick with farm work it was once again back to looking in the *Herald* to see what was around. A farm job was advertised in Hikutaia, Thames. Being open to expanding my horizons in outlying places I purchased a ticket to Thames. Not by train or car but by boat – on the coastal trader 'The Clansman'. Sailing from Auckland, she did the Thames trip in about five hours.

Not knowing what to expect, I was collected at the wharf by the farm owner and taken by car some four or five miles along the Paeroa-Kopu Road to the farm homestead. It was straight down to business upon arrival. When shown my little room, concerns mounted, as soon as I saw a wirewove bed without a mattress. Without any time for small talk I heard the instruction,

"You can change into your work attire and get ready to go out and feed the calves"

Without so much as an introduction or the offer of a cup of tea, I issued a blunt,

"No thanks, this job is not for me"

"Suit yourself," I heard him say, "You'll have to find your own way back then"

Driven to the farm I might have been, but somehow I knew I would have to take the long walk back on my own even before being told I wouldn't get a ride back. No sense in arguing with this outback old fool. The only thing to do was set off on foot for the return journey, hoping to catch up with the Clansman on its return. If the boat had already gone it would have meant nipping down on the wharf for the night and waiting until the next day. Fortunately the ship had sailed on further down the river to drop off more cargo and was on its way back. Fortune again favoured me as the ship's master saw me frantically waving from the wharf. He must have thought me somewhat odd. Still, the ship kindly pulled over to pick me up. And so a short sharp sojourn ended. Another life experience for me!

The 'Clansman' - I sailed on this boat from Auckland to Thames and then back again on the same day. Operated by The Northern Steamship Company and carrying cargo such as wool between Auckland and the Coromandel and other routes. (Source: NZ Maritime Index, 1153988, Vehicle ID, official #153 988)

Farm job number three (or four if I would consider Hikutaia a job) was to be at Takanini, again seen advertised in the *Herald*. My accommodation was a room adjourning the house. I soon felt comfortable and happy here. Dinner time found us all together around the family table which was in contrast to my experiences in Matamata. It is odd how I can recall so many details of my long life, yet in respect to this family whom I was happy to be with, much as I have searched my brain, I cannot recall the family name. I shall just have to stay with the fond memories. Here I milked 25 cows twice a day and performed other farm tasks. At the break of dawn when rounding up the cows, the farm's jersey bull had to be closely watched for he looked mean and ready to charge. Maybe he had been left in with the cows for too long! It was pleasing to get back to milking by machine and I had no problem milking by myself. The milk shed, if it could have been called a shed, consisted of just three milking bays. I know that today's sheds hold many more – they even have rotating platforms and other fancy devices.

Haymaking using horse drawn mowers turned out to be a community event. The mowers were geared, manually shifted into gear before the horses took over. The next step saw the horses drawing the spikers down the rows of cut grass. Spikers consisted of a wide row of thin steel prongs, wheels either side, the revolving spikes picking up the grass and turning it over into neat rows. Neighbours joined in with pitch forks, bundling the cut and dried hay into tradesman-like stacks, while the women dished out cream scones and tipped barley water into large white enamel cups. No teasing from adopted sons at this farm. In contrast to that, the family's youthful and attractive daughter caught my eye. That wasn't a problem but the boyfriend posed one for sure. He watched me carefully.

The family attended church on Sundays. On my day off I didn't do anything spectacular, preferring just to loll around, relaxing and reading Zane Grey westerns. I spent many an hour visualising myself riding the prairies, rounding up cattle and chasing Indians. Two of my favourite westerns included 'Riders of the Purple Sage' and 'The Last of the Plainsmen'. Another was 'Jonathon', an Indian tale, although when searching Zane Grey's published works, this title didn't show up. By the time I had journeyed through Otorohanga, Matamata and Takanini many a Zane Grey book had passed by my eyes. Indeed, I think I read most of them.

Two of the Zane Grey Westerns I read. (Source: Zane Grey' West Society-www.zgws.org)

Never losing my love of westerns, my later years appetites were satisfied with John Wayne ('The Duke') films and later still with Clint Eastwood's westerns. 'The Good, the Bad and the Ugly' being a particular favourite.

After some 12 -18 months working on the Takanini dairy farm I was suddenly told that the farm could no longer keep me. Why was I surprised? This was the second time this had happened. I had felt that things were progressing well. My immediate suspicion was that the attentions I was placing on the family's daughter influenced this decision more than anything else. More likely though, the economic climate once again would have been the major factor in the farm having to release me as a farmhand. Farming in the depression era wasn't easy. Every penny had to be accounted for.

Farm life, while I was enjoying it, wasn't going anywhere for me. Long term, I couldn't see myself owning and running my own farm. Being just a farmhand didn't allow me to have a say in any decision-making. Having given farm work three good shots it seemed that all too often I was given notice of termination and scolded, or bullied and frustrated by boyfriends. It was time to give farming away and seek a change in direction.

Changing tack wasn't to be simply a case of jumping from one job to another. A return to the apartment blocks in central Auckland where I had stayed previously for a short time was in order. The rather elderly lady proprietor (name forgotten) greeted me with an,

"Are you back again, Charlie?"

"Yes, I'm back again," I replied, thinking this greeting must have been made thousands of times before.

Having a special rapport with female genders (at least I believed I did!) a special deal was negotiated with the landlady. Or was the deal offered to all the proprietors' customers and not just to special friends?

Searching for an alternative to farm work continued. I decided to write to the Prime Minister Michael Joseph Savage asking for work. The Minister of Labour, Tim Armstrong, asked that I go and see Cyril Box, Head of Department for the New Zealand Railways. Shortly after this meeting I received an offer to work for NZ Rail in Mercer.

Hubert Thomas (Tim) Armstrong (1875–1942), is described on the Dictionary of New Zealand Biography web site as being a labourer, miner, trade unionist, politician. "Able, articulate, and occasionally abrasive, Tim Armstrong championed the rights of workers as a member of parliament from 1922 and later as a minister in the first Labour government. As minister of labour Armstrong promoted the swift improvement in pay and conditions for the country's numerous relief workers."

Receiving the confirmation in the post certainly brightened up my day. Leaving farm life behind, it was now off to the bright lights of Mercer. I anticipated a big change. Being out in the country talking to animals rather than humans was never going to be a preparation for working for Railways and gazing at giant steel locomotives. Whatever, working out on the farm had diminished in appeal for me. Still I wondered how different it would be? Was it to somehow suit the 'loner' element residing within me?

The accommodation I was given consisted of a small railway hut, sitting by itself beside the railway yard. That part was still much the same as the 'huts' I was used to on the farm. I remember how distinguished the hut looked with its reddish brown colour. Single room, single window, single bed, single one ring stove and single wash basin waited to greet me as its latest resident.

Photo of Mercer Railway Station and village. (Source: Sir George Grey Special Collections, Auckland Libraries,AWNS-18980611-4-1. Photographer – Pegler)

My new job consisted of sweeping railway platforms and assisting the girls in the railway café when they needed assistance. Ladies working in railway cafes were always called 'the girls'. They were appreciative of having a man about. Their job was to have the ham sandwiches and pies ready before passenger trains pulled in for the short refreshment stop in Mercer. The 8 minute stop became an iconic 'tradition' much like the 'six o'clock swill' in New Zealand pubs.

The scenario wonderfully told in many articles featuring stories of NZ Railway history. Here is one;

"Until 1958 Mercer railway station had refreshment rooms where passengers could purchase and hastily consume pies, sandwiches, cakes and cups of tea served in thick china cups.

Poet A.R.D Fairburn wittily commented on this fare in 'Note on NZR': 'the thought occurs to those who are entrained: the squalid tea of Mercer is not strained'.

At Christmas time I got the perk job of boning ham cuts and rolling them for slicing. Hams arrived via the Guards Van – the last train carriage. Mince, peas, pastry, sugar were kept in dedicated Railways food stores adjacent to the station. Also stored in the food store was sulphuric acid. The acid was used to top up fire extinguishers, one of my additional job responsibilities. On one particular day, sugar bags in the store were found to have been eaten away by leaking acid mistakenly stored above the food. Not a very cleaver thing to do by whoever did such a thing. Much as they tried, management could not find the culprit of this unthinking act. It wasn't me!

With the railway huts being basic in design and without provisions for hot water or the luxury of a hot bath, Jim Irvine, a railway repairer kindly invited me to take hot baths at his home. These invitations were gratefully accepted. It was a sad day when news came through that Jim had been killed in a shunting accident at Huntly.

Because working took up most of my time, there were few opportunities to develop real friendships. A landmark building in Mercer was the Mercer pub. Not lawfully permitted to frequent the pub, much as I may have liked too, I thought it best to wait a year or two before I tried to sneak in. I did not know it yet but I was to establish a connection with the Sunnex family, an association destined to begin at Maungaturoto and conclude with my return from the war in 1943. There is more to tell about this later. Tom Sunnex became the proprietor of the Mercer pub during latter days when I was stationed at Maungaturoto. Tom had two young daughters, Joan and Betty.

The Mercer Hotel – the proprietor of the pub at one stage was Tom Sunnex – the father of sisters Betty and Joan. (Source: Auckland War Memorial Museum Mercer, showing River View Private Hotel – B9247)

The Railways received notification that an employee was killed in an automobile accident after hitting a bridge at Maungaturoto. As a result of this tragedy I was asked to go there. Actually there was no choice, it was go or not have a job. The Mercer café girls complained bitterly, not wanting to lose their 'meat slicer', but progress called and off I went – to Maungaturoto having spent two years at Mercer.

MAUNGATUROTO

At nearly 20 years of age and knowing nothing of the place I was heading to, I took the train and headed north. Whatever pioneering spirit resided in me would be tested in this isolated outpost in rural New Zealand. I soon settled into my new lodgings – a one room railway hut furnished with a small stove, a bunk bed with a mattress, a curtain and a radio aerial. Washing had to be done in the washroom located away from the hut. Cold water only – again! For company there were three other huts. One hut reserved for the bridge inspector and one for the railway shunter, a man named Pat Hickey (later to be my Best Man). The bridge inspector arrived on his motorised jigger once every two or three months. He would stay in his hut for two or three days.

Without a bike or any other mode of transport and distance between my little hut and civilisation I decided to spend some of my hard earned wages. With no real vices and with ladies both out of sight and out of reach, or so it seemed, I splashed out and with my hard earned spare cash purchased a Model A Ford Roadster from the only garage in town – the one across the road. She was the latest two-seater model. A distinctive feature of my new car was its rounded style boot. Bought second hand she became loved from the day she came into my possession.

Around Maungaturoto cars were scarce, with few car owners about. A sure way to gain popularity was to become an owner. My star soon brightened amongst the local fraternity. If not everyone knew me before, they did now. Even the engine stoker at Maungaturoto got to know who I was. He became the first to borrow my 'Gertie'. Petrol prices at the time were steady, not influenced by oil price fluctuations as they are today. Putting a gallon in my tank cost me the grand sum of one shilling and nine pence. Amongst the oil company brands I remember being advertised in the 1930s were Big Tree, Caltex and Mexico.

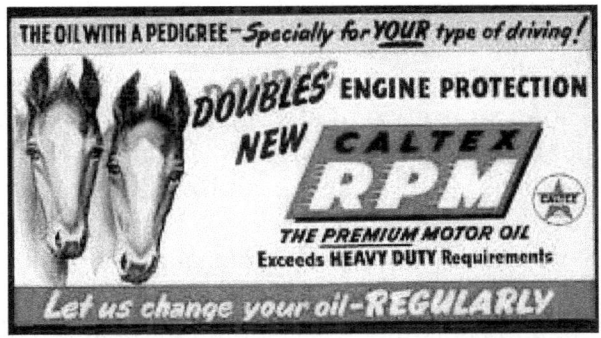

You could expect advertisements even in the 1920s and 1930s. (Source: NZ 1930s Caltex Oil RPM Blotter Card, advertising blotter card)

Petrol was gravity fed as early model cars did not have petrol pumps. To start the car the spark gap first had to be set, the spark plug setting being positioned beside the steering wheel. Next, you took a trip around to the front of the car and grabbing the crank handle you had to make sure that the first crank was turned slowly before giving it a full crank. If this was not done correctly a broken wrist could easily have resulted.

My Model A was similar to this one. (Source - John MacDonald, Summerville, Nova Scotia Canada)

My sleek Ford Model A relieved me of £170. Considering I earned £3 that would be the equivalent of around $30,000 in today's terms. Having the car allowed me to travel dusty and metalled roads to Mt Eden, Auckland, once a month. I would usually leave early on Saturday morning. Staying in Auckland overnight, I would sometimes attend the pictures on Sunday night before making the two to three hour return trip to Maungaturoto, finally crawling into my railway hut bed at about 1 am in the morning.

It may be difficult to visualise the landscapes and road conditions of the early 1930s if you have not travelled them yourself and your only appreciation of them has come from what you may have seen in historical photographs. Riverhead roads clogged and rutted with clay after rain, ambushed my wheels, pulling them into deep groves in the road. Such conditions did not make for trip highlights, however I look back on them now with some sense of morbid pride, having survived such intrepid journeys. Considering I was travelling on my lonesome, getting stuck provided few options but for me to get out of the car, rain or not and vandalise some tea tree (plentiful around Riverhead). The tea tree (or manuka) was laid out around the wheels to provide traction and allow escape.

A special feature of the sleek Model A Ford was that its design allowed you to observe the metal roads just below the floorboards. Had air conditioning been available it would not have been particularly useful anyway. Hand in hand with this view you could also see the white hot exhaust system working away and providing a little interior heat.

My first car came to a sad end when the beloved thing had to be set free – handed over to Ernie to sell for me when I departed for war overseas. Apparently, Ernie sold it, as far as I can remember for some soap and foot powder. The arrangements we made between us were certainly loose on specific agreements, lacking in detail about how I would be financially compensated. My 48 base piano accordion was traded along with my car. Ernie would have known what happened to the monies involved, or is it possible that he did not really care or lost track of things? Anyway, I never really pursued the issue and on my return from the war it was left 'as is'. From my viewpoint, my thinking at the time led me to believe that I might not return from the war. I was not fatalistic but I did have a realisation that I could die fighting there. That coupled with the excitement of getting on a troopship sailing for another country meant that I could unreservedly say to Ernie, "I'll leave the handling of the car and piano accordion to you, please do what you think is best with them".

Working for the Railways in Maungaturoto meant that I had to service the trains at the station platform as they passed through. Not many were seen, maybe three on a busy day. As the trains came in the engine driver would lean out of the engine and click the 'tablet' onto a standing mechanical arm. I would then unclip the tablet and deliver it to the station office, placing it on the telegraph machine, thus confirming with Auckland that the train had reached Maungaturoto. The station master would then exit the office and with his flag wave the train on. In those days computerised systems had not even been thought of.

Steam train and locomotive (by engine shed) on parallel lines at Maungaturoto. (Source: A P Godber Collection, Alexander Turnbull Library, Ref APG-1137-1/2-G)

With so few trains passing through the station this part of my job occupied only a few hours of the day. Maungaturoto station was not like a metropolitan city station buzzing with people, she was a tiny rural station, stuck out in the wilderness of northern New Zealand. To make sure I was useful I would help out in the Railway canteen. My experiences gained working at the Mercer Railways stood me in good stead. A typical day for me involved working from 6 am until around 3 pm. The canteen employed four or five service people, café girls as they were called, and was run by the head girl Mavis Wakeland. The Maungaturoto menu offered much the same as Mercer's did. A menu New Zealand Railways became so well known for - a cup of tea served in railway porcelain and the great NZ Railways pie.

Versatility was my second name and I would sweep the platform when the pies were in the cooker. Stocks of 50lb flour bags were held in the railway store. Mince was sourced from the butcher located across the road. Dried peas were sent from Auckland. Stocks had to be sufficient to service the demands as clients rushed from the trains in pressing numbers for their pie and tea – all to be completed within eight minutes or they risked missing the train.

An A class locomotive No. 582, with the Maungaturoto-Auckland train, 1933. (Source: NZETC – Photo, H. Bennett, NZ Railways Magazine, Vol 9, Issue 12)

I got on well with the girls at Mercer and it was no different at Maungaturoto. In a short time I became friendly with all the café girls and struck up a particularly keen friendship with Joan Sunnex. I would not have minded at all if the friendship had developed further, however Joan wasn't so keen on serious relationships as she had definite intentions on becoming a nurse. Maybe so as to not disappoint me, she suggested that I may like her sister who happened to live in Mercer (at the Mercer pub). Not long after, Betty Sunnex came up to Maungaturoto to work in the café along with her sister Joan. My friendship with Betty went along fine and I invited her on a trip home to Mt Eden to meet dad Charles and Annie. A week or two later we travelled to Auckland in the Model A. Charles and Annie were impressed by Betty, telling me that she was a 'beauty'. The friendship continued until I left for war. As told later, I sent Betty gifts from Egypt, however on my return to New Zealand all was lost – Betty had run off with a 'Yank'. That was not nice at all! I should have taken the barman's job Betty's father Tom had offered me! I might have had a better chance that way.

Railway Station Tearooms – 1946 – eight minutes was all the time you got! (Source: Alexander Turnbull Library-'Busy railway tearoom', PAColl-5927-52. W.G.Weigel). www.nzhistory.net.nz/media/photo/busy-railway-tearooms)

When the trains pulled in for their timed stop and passengers hastily ate their pies and sammies, I would gather all the empty cups and saucers left around the carriages using an old kerosene tin. Gathering as many I could (eight minute stops only!) they were taken to the shed and packed in special boxes for return to Auckland. A waybill had to made out. Over the years many railway cups disappeared never to be seen again, kept as souvenirs or for other purposes. This 'collection' job was not a job I had at Mercer. It wasn't long before I earned the nickname of 'Cups King', which did not have quite the same meaning as the nickname given to Bart Cummings, champion race horse trainer and 'Cups King' of Australian Racing, many of whose horses I had backed, mostly unsuccessfully.

One of my tougher jobs was shovelling coal. Shunt wagons (or LAs) would pull up and be parked beside the woolshed. Contractors supplied sacks which were tossed up onto the top of the wagons. The sacks were filled with coal, up to 80 kilograms per sack. Once filled the sacks would be picked up by a two wheeled transporter sled and taken over a wide plank across to the woolshed landing. The woolshed may have been called a wool shed but often it would be filled with superphosphate fertiliser or in this case, by coal.

Maungaturoto was a lonely place but I developed some sort of affinity for this northern station. People and communities, where ever they are, seem to make their own fun and Maungaturoto folk were no different. Keg parties were easy to arrange and they were popular. There was no trouble in booking the local pub or local homes as venues. This was a small but close knit community. Most of the homes in the area were Railway homes, typically with three bedrooms and tenanted by engine drivers, station masters and railway foremen. Railway workers were allocated railway 'huts.' Local house parties were simple but fun. Girls would bring food and gentlemen brought kegs of beer. Sing songs accompanied by piano or guitar made for enjoyable evenings (and nights). Then there were the wind up gramophones often spinning the Victor label.

Once a month, a dance night was held in the railway hall. The hall was attached to the railway refreshment rooms, and was typical of dance halls seen in so many New Zealand rural towns. It was a rather large building with high ceilings, wooden floors and a piano geared up for country dances, tucked away in a corner. Dance night provided opportunities for townsmen to chase the refreshment girls. Not too much encouragement was needed. More than a few associations and shenanigans started off at these dances. One or two revellers were seen carrying on in the long tall rye grass outside. Lucky to have resident locals playing on the saxophone and on the piano, the dance floor was never empty as waltzes, foxtrots and jives tested heart rates. So enjoyable were these get-togethers that I shall always remember them.

The Maungaturoto pub had the privilege of becoming the first tavern I frequented. Alcoholic beverages became one of my preferred regular companions. Occasional trips were made to Whangarei to do some shopping but also to visit the Settler's Hotel on Bank Street.

Building the Maungaturoto Hotel – 1902 – visited on a few occasions. (Source: Northland History.blogspot.co.nz – Back Roads – The Scandalous Maungaturoto Hotel 1902 Part 2)

Being under the influence risked the odd misdemeanours being committed especially in Maungaturoto which could not claim to provide an exciting range of entertainment. On one particular occasion while having a few beers after work, feeling bored and not looking forward to the same old dinner, we suddenly struck on a bright idea when one of the lads suggested, "Let's go check out our cantankerous old neighbour's chooks; we may be able to find ourselves a few eggs."

It didn't take much more prompting before we set off for the neighbour's farm. The decision made easier since all agreed the farmer to be mean spirited and unsociable. Once the eggs were gathered and our lookout waved the all clear we returned to base.

The next morning we bowled up to the café with 20 or so eggs.

"Here we are girls," we offered, "how about you fry these up for a healthy breakfast."

So we had eggs for breakfast, no questions asked.

In my hut I had a crystal set and so had contact with a wider world. I couldn't pick up much but I listened intently to whatever broadcast my little set managed to tune into.

Without Foodtown or Countdown stores, shopping choices were limited. Being so convenient, and not because Railways offered staff discounts, lunch and dinner often consisted of the good old Railway pie and sometimes ham sandwiches. Healthy eating passed me by. My stove in the hut got little use.

There were two unoccupied huts at the yard and I was entrusted with the keys for these. With people paying occasional visits or just happening to be passing through, a few couples thought it might be useful to make use of the huts for 'love-ins'. That the huts might be used for such purposes was never the intention of the New Zealand Railways. On one occasion, I was asked by a desperate looking couple whom I had never met before,

"Kind sir, we have been told that you are the owner of the keys for that little unoccupied hut over yonder. We have struggled all day travelling here, would you mind if we bedded down just for the night?" Succumbing to my natural kindness, I handed over the keys. "Just the one night," I said. I knew full well that if I was found out I would get into trouble for breaking the rules and passing on the keys to strangers. True enough, my misdemeanour was found out and the keys were removed from my care!

One of the few sporting activities offered in the area was tennis, played on the adjacent Railways-owned asphalt tennis courts. A keen contest was always had amongst us, particularly with Pat Hickey, the head shunter who occupied one of the other railway huts. My aim in our local competitions was to always get into the top six as they would go on to play in local area tournaments. Pat and I formed the Maungaturoto doubles combination. Pat was later to be my best man at my wedding. We entered local area competitions whenever we could, such as at Makarau. Doubles and singles were played.

Life was good at Maungaturoto and probably could have drifted on forever. But life is also unpredictable, and situations emerge demanding responses. The start of World War II changed everything for me.

Having heard of the Prime Minister Michael Savage's stirring request for New Zealand men to volunteer for military service, I felt his message was aimed directly at me, his words about 'where Britain stands we stand' and particularly those 'we are a band of brothers' got me keenly motivated to be one of the brothers. Having already worked on dairy farms I appreciated that most of our export trade (80%) was going to mother England. Apart from that newspapers exhorted New Zealand men to fight for their country and radio broadcasts extolled the same message. I heard that elsewhere, in other towns, loudspeakers on the roofs of recruiting vans made sure the message was heard in the streets and that doctors visited workplaces for on-the-spot medical exams. (www.nzhistory.net.nz)

I decided to enlist and sent off an application letter. Upon receiving the reply from the New Zealand Army, my goodbyes had to be said to Maungaturoto. In good old New Zealand tradition a farewell party was arranged for me and three fellow volunteers. Forty five gallons of beer made sure the occasion offered plenty of loud and joyous celebrations. Jim Mason, Jim Bracegirdle and Don Debey, a junior shunter, were bid farewell along with me. Jim Bracegirdle became a gunner in a Halifax bomber crew. He died in an air battle over Germany.

Enlisting was not questioned by those who volunteered. For many, a sense of duty became the simple persuader and for others it was even simpler, for them it was just 'the thing to do'. The sense of adventure struck a cord with my wandering spirit. We put our names down without asking questions. Of one thing there would be little doubt and that is that few volunteers would ever have clearly visualised or understood the realities of the war they were about to experience. A few voices spelling out warnings did surface. One of these came from the railway bridge inspector, who tried to warn me,

"Son," he said, "this war you are going to is neither a holiday nor a walk in the park. This war is a very serious business indeed. You will need to have your wits about you, and please try to think straight."

Much as I have tried to recall the inspector's name, his name eludes me. I very much respected that man. I had wondered if he experienced war but I did not ask him. Maybe being of middle age, he had had some experience of war in WW1. While I believed what the inspector was saying, I didn't really appreciate the details of it, since I had not had any experience of a real battlefield – an exercise sitting on a horse in Whangarei, tent pegging, as close as I got to the real thing! Many a time I have reflected on what the inspector said to me. His words having added impact since his conversations with me were valued and appreciated.

However the decision was made and there was no going back.

CHAPTER 4

THE WAR YEARS

POP – TROOPER 21939

Four years of my life had been spent working in Maungaturoto. I could quite happily have gone on working there since I felt comfortable where I was, however the call for volunteers to fight to defend freedom and the opportunity to go overseas held a greater pull over me than staying on at Maungaturoto. I felt I had to go.

It was while working here that a fellow railway worker invited me to join in with a Territorial Army group. With plenty of time on my hands, the invitation was duly accepted. The Territorials held monthly army practice exercises. A camp was arranged to be held at Kensington Park, Whangarei. Focal points of this camp were the horses and tent pegging exercises. Many of the Territorials from around the district owned their own 'hacks' which they brought along to the camp. For those not having a horse, one would be loaned to them. You took your luck on this, as you would most likely be loaned a draught horse. Tent pegging was similar to medieval jousting and consisted of horsemen charging at tent pegs placed in the ground. With spear in hand, the aim was to stab the peg. The peg was meant to simulate a poor old human being. The superior experience of some of the horsemen soon showed. The inexperience of others did too, especially those riders loaned draught horses, as they were observed massaging their sore bums! This whole exercise seemed to be a bit of a throwback to ancient WW1 practices and many wondered what relevance such exercises had as to what was about to happen in WW2. Maybe there was a little lack of vision here as the Territorial commander at the end of training excitedly suggested to me, "With the army training you have had young man, you will know what to do."

I was not so sure about that!

Tent pegging – imagine me on a draught horse doing this! (Source: www.googl.co.nz- rachel96.weeby.com/tent-pegging.html)

War had broken out and calls went out for volunteers. Having experience with the Territorials behind me, a questioning mind and a roving spirit, these things swayed me to make the decision to join the war effort. The radio news service and newspapers carried daily news reports covering international developments. Editorials spoke of supporting Mother England and its allies as the war mobilisation momentum increased. Around the railway yards discussions often swung around to talk about war. Many opinions were offered and they weren't all in agreement. All of this forced me to answer my own question of 'What should I do? How can I be part of this?'

After enlisting in Whangarei, I made a call to Cyril Box, the boss of Railways in Auckland informing him of my enlistment. Not happy at all, Mr Box remonstrated,

"I can't wait for you to come back from the war you know" I knew that, but I didn't believe he needed to say it quite like that.

His curtly said, "I can't guarantee you anything you know", was hardly heard.

'Recruitment poster, 1940' (Source: Ministry for Culture and Heritage site. Reference: NZRLS – 004)

An enjoyable association with Maungaturoto was coming to an end. At the same time the Prime Minister, Michael Savage asked New Zealand men to offer themselves as volunteers to fight for freedom. Earlier, becoming eligible to vote, I had voted for Michael Savage, the then leader of the Labour Government. So listening to the Prime Minister's call I felt it was right for me to freely and willingly accept the call to arms.

Recruitment poster (Source: Military history of New Zealand during World War II – Wikipedia, the free encyclopaedia)

It was some three months later that I heard of my acceptance into the New Zealand Army. On the 12th January, 1940, leaving Maungaturoto behind, I drove south to the Papakura Army Base, which was to be my new home for the next three months. Our training in preparation for war consisted of; practising 303 rifle drills, route marches along the main roads of Papakura and Bren gun training. There was also some training with WW1 Vickers Machine guns but these caused frustrations due to their regular jamming.

Papakura Army barracks – 1940s

Powell, Arthur Walter, 1893-1970: Photograph of World War II soldiers of the 3rd Echelon, clearing out their hut at Papakura Military Camp, Auckland,(ca, 4 Oct 1940) (Source: Reference Number: PAColl-8847)

New Zealand was to provide an Expeditionary Force of one division, under Major-General Bernard Freyberg. This force became known as the 2nd New Zealand Expeditionary Force and the division, initially as the New Zealand Division. It was made up of; 5th Infantry Brigade (21st, 22nd, 23rd and the 28th (Maori) Infantry Battalions), 5th Field Regiment, 7th Anti-tank Regiment (31 & 32 Batteries), and C Squadron of the Divisional Cavalry (my unit), elements of 6th Brigade HQ (being sent out to prepare training programs for the Third Echelon) and the 7th Field (Engineer) Company. (Source: Avalanche Press-2nd New Zealand Division in WWII. Part 1: From Formation to Dispatch Overseas. By Brian Knipple, February 2006)

With training completed at Papakura, arrangements were made for troops to congregate in Wellington prior to sailing to Egypt, but not before the final 'passing out' parade happened in front of mums and dads and lots of photographers. The 2nd Echelon gathered in Wellington along with the 9th Maori Battalion to board troopships destined to sail to Egypt. However, due to Italy's entry into the war, the 2nd Echelon was diverted to Britain via Cape Town, South Africa, and did not reach Egypt until March 1941. A total of 6838 personnel were allocated to four ships. Over 2000 were assigned to the ship I was put on - the Aquitania.

In my uniform – on desert leave - photo taken in Egypt

Sailing to War

'Troopship Aquitania ready to depart' (news clip)
'On 2 May 1940, after three months of training, the Second Echelon of the NZ Expeditionary Force sailed from Wellington aboard the distinguished luxury liner Aquitania. After being joined by other troop ships in Australian ports, the convoy sailed for Egypt but diverted to England, where New Zealand's First Echelon had already established its base. But on 15 May, four days after leaving Fremantle, the ships were diverted to South Africa – intelligence reports suggested that Italy was about to declare war on the Allies and potentially blockade the Red Sea.' (Source: Call to Arms/28th Maori Battalion)

Image shows the Aquitania in Wellington Harbour in 1940, when this Cunard White Star liner first visited New Zealand to load troops for the Middle East. (Source: 'The Aquitania in Wellington Harbour', URL: www.nzhistory.net.nz/media/photo/ (Ministry for Culture and Heritage), 1940)

My Life – the Meanderings of Pop Knill

The Aquitania in all its glory as a Cunard Line passenger ship. (Copyright http://www.clydebuiltships.co.uk and http://www.clydesite.co.uk)

Extract from Web Search

The Aquitania was a converted passenger ship, Cunard Line. She was the last surviving four funnelled ocean liner. Launched on the 21st April 1913 she served for 36 years. After each of the two World Wars she served in she was returned to passenger service. With a crew of 972 and capable of carrying 2200 passengers she carried nearly 400,000 soldiers sailing 500,000 miles in her 8 years of military work. In her entire career she steamed 3 million miles in 450 voyages carrying 1.2 million passengers. The Aquitania was scrapped at Faslane, Scotland in 1950. (Source – Wikipedia)

Cape Town and on to England

After reaching Cape Town on 26 May 1940, the Aquitania anchored at a nearby naval base. The Pākehā troops were soon given shore leave, but due to South Africa's policies of racial segregation, the men of the Māori Battalion were kept on the ship for four days. An interesting site to observe while leaning over the ship's rails sailing into the South African port were the flying fish scuttling through the sea. Many soldiers took the opportunity to do some sightseeing, visiting Table Mountain and other sites but for me and some of my mates sightseeing didn't hold much of an attraction so we decided to go off and sample the local brew instead.

Back on board after shore leave the Aquitania sailed on its final leg to England, arriving in July 1940. During the voyage on the South Atlantic we saw flashes in the sky and floating debris passing by, raising concerns of an imminent attack. The German cruiser 'Scharnhorst' had been attacking a convoy of Allied ships. Having the battleship, the Ramillies, plus seven other ships escorting the Aquitania certainly negated the fear a little.

And so I had my first experience of witnessing enemy fire power and feeling apprehensive about being attacked.

War Time Events Book

When work on this project was nearing completion, Pop pulled out of one of his drawers what looked to be an exercise book. The 'Events Book' was a handwritten record of events during the war and includes some poems. This book, with the German swastika on the cover, contained contributions from Pop and fellow soldiers. The poems do not contain a glorification of wartime battles but are a soldier's expression of what life was like near to or under fire, the conditions he lived in, and the feelings of loss for dead comrades and his distant home. Excerpts have been used through this chapter to help provide timelines and to highlight events. Note that this Events Book, as we have called it, differs from the official Soldier's Handbook provided by the army to each soldier for record purposes.

The following timeline provides an overview of my movements during my involvement in WWII. The countries and places I went to are identified here;

> Jan. 12-1-40 Went into Papakura camp (for overseas.)
> May. 2-5-40 Left for overseas from Wellington (and Ech.) in Troopship "Aquitania"
> July 27-7-40 Arrived safely in England
> January 2-1-41 Left England for Middle East
> March 5-3-41 Arrived at Suez, Egypt.
> March 23.3.41 Left Egypt for Greece
> March 15.3.41 Arrived safe at Piraeas
> April 28.4.41 Left Greece for Crete
> May 2.5.41 Arrived back in Egypt
> Lybian Campaign I
> " " II
> Jan. 23.1.43 Arrived Tripoli — III
> June 15-6-43 Left Middle East for NZ.
> July 12.7.43 Arrived safely at Wellington NZ
> Sept. 25-9-43 — Election day (was engaged)
> Oct 11-10-43 Was medically graded w.p.—J.
> Nov. 27-11-43 Was Honorably discharged from The 2nd NZEF.
> Troopships we travelled on were
> 44.000 tons "Aquitania" to England
> "Dutchess of Bedford" back to Middle East
> 19.000 tons.

Pop's timeline (Source: Extract from wartime Events Book)

England

With the original intention of sailing to Egypt thwarted by the Italian situation, the Aquitania eventually docked at Port Greenock after sailing up the Clyde, England, in July 1940. Our New Zealand troops settled into their army base amongst strands of pine trees in Aldershot, Southern England, only some 10-15 miles from London.

Delayed in reaching Egypt for the time being, it was here that I saw my first action of sorts. In the distance I could see the night sky being lit up as London was being bombed by German bombers. Coventry also suffered from the German bombing, although it did not seem to be a strategic target. One or two lone German bombers unloaded a few bombs around Aldershot. The next day saw me helping the New Zealand contingent dig trenches 10ft deep in anticipation of further bombing raids. We had not been given any training in how a trench should be dug. Had we known that a trench half as deep would have been just as effective we could have saved all that energy. The experience of being bombed by German fighter planes amongst Aldershot's trees was not one to fondly treasure. German air force fighters were attacking British targets, mainly airfields. As we read in the papers, the bombing of London was having dramatic effects on London citizens, shaken by air raid sirens and frequently having to rush to bomb shelters.

Given a week's leave, I along with two of my comrades took a train to Edinburgh, Scotland, to get away from things to do with the war. As often happened in many countries throughout the war years, families invited soldiers into their homes. In Edinburgh I was lucky enough to stay with a Scottish family after a young lady met me at the train station. Her father was a Scottish constable so no mucking around here! I discovered this truth when I walked into the house and saw a police helmet behind a door.

Curious, I asked her "would your father happen to be a cop?"

"Please do not call my father a cop," she replied.

I assumed he was but did not ask again.

Attractive as she was, there was no chance of any thoughts of romance since the young lady had a boyfriend, albeit he happened to be overseas. The family made me welcome, providing me with a refreshing break from digging trenches, living in tin huts and shivering from the English winter cold.

This photo was taken in Aldershot, England while on leave. Two (Pommie) comrades from 'C' Squadron - one of my comrades above is Len Tru.

On a further leave excursion, I had another chance to travel out of town, this time to Glasgow by train, staying in a small motel style apartment. A little of Scotland visited. With leave over and having returned to our Aldershot base, training recommenced with route marches again the norm as was training with Bren guns and Bren carriers. The British supplied the NZ Army with second hand Bren carriers fitted with V8 engines. These required reconditioning and were taken to a nearby ex Ford factory, for this work to be done. The plant employed both men and women mechanics. Once reconditioned the Bren carriers were loaded onto ships ready to sail in convoy to Egypt. All this work came to nought when German U-boats sunk the ship transporting the Bren carriers. That must have hurt!

Maadi Camp - Egypt

After spending five months in England, on 2nd of January, 1941, our NZ 2nd Echelon left for the Middle East. Sailing around Africa on the Duchess of Bedford, we arrived in Suez, Egypt on the 5th March 1941. Base was to be established at Maadi Camp which had earlier been chosen in preference to a second option.

Our first stay at Maadi would be for less than two weeks, however it was our base and we would be coming back here from time-to-time as the war progressed. It was enough time to get to know a little about Maadi and Cairo only a few kilometres away.

Canadian Pacific Lines "Duchess of Bedford" (Source: www.simlonpc.co.uk)

I understood that General Freyberg, upon arriving in Egypt was offered the choice of two camp sites. One was on the banks of the Suez Canal, the second was at Maadi. He had little hesitation in selecting Maadi. It was suited to training and only minutes from Cairo. Maadi was to be New Zealand's main overseas base for six years. Freyberg, a man of many talents, not least his swimming ability, had a 'bath' or what we call a swimming pool measuring 30 x 10 meters built in the desert, a kilometre or two outside of Maadi camp. Maadi also had its own picture theatre – the "Shufti Shaftos".

The films shown there were very old and in atrocious condition. More often than not the projector would break down. Freyberg along with his wife established the New Zealand Club in Cairo – a place where off-duty soldiers could relax a bit, get decent meals and a drink (see later photo).

Maadi Camp (description from WWII website)

Maadi Camp, stretching out in the desert about eight miles from Cairo, was built on a plateau overlooking the Nile Valley.

It was something of a disillusionment. No one had quite expected a base camp (to all intents and purposes) out in a friendly desert, or had realized that the desert was such a colourless and depressing waste of sand. Romantic pictures of golden, rolling sand hills, were soon dispelled by hard reality, and although, later, men were to come to look on Maadi Camp as representing comfort and civilization, at first encounter the prospect of living under what then seemed such cheerless conditions was far from encouraging. The only feature to break the monotony of the surroundings was a lined and eroded escarpment beyond the camp boundaries to the south and east, while westwards in the hazy distance were age old Pyramids. There was not a tree, a bush, or any splash of living green in the camp to relieve the drab monotony of desert.

Maadi Camp (Source: Alexander Turnbull Library. Ref. DA-11253. Photo – George Bull)

The camp was a haphazard assembly of large square tents (EPIPs they were called), smaller reddish brown tents, and huts of wood or stone. More huts were being built, "Wogs' (sic) working at them, slowly, to a monotonous chant by one of their number, while camel trains carrying building materials strode leisurely through the camp. The huts were used mainly for officers, cookhouses, mess rooms or stores, and men's sleeping quarters were mainly in tents (although I remember being allocated mud huts). Erecting the tents was a major task as the rocky plateau was covered with only a few inches of sand. Camouflaged to blend with the sand, the tents spread over the desert for a considerable area, later to grow to several square miles. Later on, the building of NAAFIs (you could buy sweets, chocolates here), the YMCA, and the Lowry Hut added comfortable amenities.

Source = (J.B.McKinny, Medical Units of 2 NZEF in Middle East and Italy, 1952. Chapters 3-4). www.ourstory.info/library/4-ww2/NZmed/nzmed02/ht

In the early stages of being at Maadi I remember camels carrying giant bags of dirt or mud as they would bring their cargo to the building sites. Here the mud would be moulded in large tin moulds before being used on the walls.

Good old khaki bloomers were the required fashion here, blooming out around the legs (hence their name). Being as resourceful as we were, some of the men had their 'bloomers' shortened in Cairo. Each man was issued with two pair – made in India, quality unknown. We were expected to look after our gear.

Native tailors in one of Maadi's streets make minor alterations to the uniforms of New Zealanders from the nearby camp. (Source: World War II - Photograph - by G Kaye. Source: Alexander Turnbull Library. Ref. DA-03863-F)

Cairo was situated only a few kilometres from Maadi base. Leave was offered generously – 50% on week nights and 80% on Saturday afternoon and then after church parade on Sundays. Soldiers taking leave, would travel three miles by truck to the camp's train station named Helwan and then by diesel train from Maadi to Bab-el-Louk station in the heart of Cairo. In Cairo there was shopping for gifts to send home (see later where I describe sending stockings home to Betty in Mercer, the lady who disappeared upon my return to New Zealand).

The official soldier's handbook – I received this at Papakura – it went everywhere I went during my war service.

My book of soldier's rules – basically my introduction to army life. A fore runner of what was going to be expected of me. Some of the more interesting ones were;

- Conduct yourself on all occasions as a soldier and a gentleman

- Obey all orders cheerfully and avoid bad language and 'grousing' both of which create a bad influence amongst your comrades. If you have a genuine complaint to make submit it to your immediate commander. Disobedience of orders is a very serious offence.
- Keep yourself fit, avoid excesses of stimulants and above all remember the very serious dangers of illicit sexual intercourse, against which you are specially warned in the interests of your future health and happiness.

As soldiers, we found the demands of training and being a soldier was enough discipline in itself. We understood the need for rules but we also felt the hierarchy had shown its intent, written down in every soldier's personal handbook.

What were we soldiers to do with our pay? We could spend it on leave in Cairo or Alexandria or save it to take home. My soldier mates would say they were perpetually hard up. The suspicion held by others was that most of it was spent, or maybe all of it was spent! There were all those delights that Cairo offered. The servicemen's club, beer bars, movies and cabarets not to mention houses of ill repute. I behaved myself, in Cairo I recall seeing 'Gone with the Wind' and Irvin Berlin's – 'Hells-a-Poppin'.

My Life – the Meanderings of Pop Knill

War pay – paid on leave – spending money for Cairo. *[Note: Pop recalls being paid approximately £1/week however gauging by entries above it may have been per fortnight. Notice a few 'gaps' e.g. no entries for December 1941. Also note the entry of £15 7 9 in January.]*

One hundred 'ackers' equalled an Egyptian pound, or five ackers equalled five shillings being the exchange rate. A week's pay was around 10 shillings. ('Acker' was the army term used for piaster; one acker equalled one piastre and 100 piastres equalled one Egyptian pound.)

It was in Cairo where fortune tellers offered their specific brand of entertainment or 'service'. My mate, a believer in supernatural things egged me on, "Charlie mate, these fortune tellers I am told are good, we must hear what they have to say."

Considering a visit as a bit of a lark, I half reluctantly said, "Right, but I hope we get something worthwhile out of it, so you had better be correct."

Off we went to see what the future might hold for us. Into the fortune teller's den I went and before the 'learned' gentleman I sat.

Egyptian Street Fortune Teller Has Two Women Engrossed in His Soothsaying
(Source: Art.com - Giclee Print - item #: 4058953839A)

He was an Egyptian gentleman who considered himself possessed of Solomon's wisdom having studied the bible.

"Come along, sit down my friends, I see you wish to know your fortune."

"We do" we both replied at the same time.

I couldn't make up my mind if this was something genuine.

With a stick he scribbled lines and circles in the sand as one would read palms. The prediction went something like –

"You will return home and see a big crowd, two women and a celebration."

"Where will this happen?" I asked "Will this happen soon?"

The fortune teller rambled on a little more but offered few facts containing any substance.

Having to part with five pilasters did not initially impress me. However, years after I returned from the war I changed my tune a little. I came to see the teller's prediction to mean the dance hall at Khyber Pass and the two women to be Lorraine and Eileen and the celebration to be our eventual marriage. Some may think that such predictions would simply relate to one of the more common experiences of life and thus be a logical prediction to make. The 'mate' who had led me to the fortune teller was Len Tru. We had been together on the Aquitania when we sailed off to war from

Wellington. I had a lot of respect for Len, so much so that Len, my oldest son was named after him. A distinctive feature of Len's was his golden front tooth which I reckoned many a lady graduated too. Not for the first time in my life, Len was another comrade who became lost in time and another friend that featured in my often reoccurring thoughts of 'I wonder whatever happened to ..?' I still think of Len Tru when I ring Len, my son in Australia.

New Zealand Forces Club, Cairo. A rest and recreation facility for NZ soldiers. Organised and arranged by Freyburg's wife. I am at the end of the middle row – right. This group is part of my unit – 'C' Squadron. The 'A' and 'B' Squadrons were already in Egypt when I was first stationed in England.

Questions people often ask about being in foreign countries are 'how did the local Egyptians react to the foreign 'invasion' of Maadi?' General consensus suggests that Maadi Egyptians were mostly anti-British. The older generation would not demonstrate signs of resentment in public but tended to express their feelings in home gatherings. Younger Egyptians were more open and radical about their resentment of the 'inglizi'. A few local men married British wives; such marriages were viewed by certain snooty English gentlemen as a let-down and being below their class. Whatever views the Egyptians may have held in respect to these foreigners in their country, a number of them were certainly expert 'pick pockets'. I can vouch for that.

Showing off newly issued gear while on leave (either Cairo or Alexandria).

At the camp accommodation tents were put up, but I remember more about the mud huts. The huts were long with up to 30 men sleeping on beds of straw. Erected by Egyptian workers (wogs), huts were made of mud and straw bound together. Water was held in gazerers also made of mud and holding about 20 litres of water. The gazerers kept the water cool - a necessity in the Egyptian desert. The square, brownish coloured tents accommodated four to six men each. After taking showers in the camp shower block, we would saturate our towels and place the towels around our heads before heading back to our tents. By the time we reached the tent our towels were already bone dry, such was the heat and dryness. Our tent beds were called 'paillasses' a sort of canvas lilo filled with straw (likely Indian made). When occasional dust storms swept across the camp we would quickly take refuge in our tents.

Barracks at Maadi. The barracks remembered but not so much the tents. (Source: ww2 New Zealand Officers photos Egypt & North Africa (1939-42)-#10)

Training started in earnest at Maadi. Slowly at first, a mile every day, marching in army boots, thick socks, Bombay bloomers, thin shirts and polystyrene helmets. Each day a few miles were added to the distance until a total of 14 miles was reached. Sweat flowed freely down the back and into the shorts, excess pounds were soon shed and those who tended to be thin got even thinner. I, being one of the thin ones, held my shape. Marching was hot, sweaty and painful but relieved somewhat when the Army band played our weary troops back into camp. Marches began at 2 pm, since the sun was hottest in the morning. Our unit usually returned at around 6 pm just in time for us to pick up our 'dixies' and line up for dinner.

Training soon moved onto using Bren guns. The Bren carriers (vehicles shaped like tanks but with the top halves cut off them) destined to replace those sunk on the ocean in transit from England had not yet arrived. With army organisation and planning being what it was, having insufficient ammunition for firing practice ended up being one more frustration we all had to put up with. As a consequence target practice was limited to just single rounds followed by a short burst of fire. The training exercise finished with us having to clean our guns using ropes attached to a rod and then using a cleaning plug of cloth pulled through the barrel. The Maadi training exercises were similar to those practiced at the Papakura

Army base back in New Zealand. Mind you, while the training exercises were similar, the conditions were not. Lying down on the desert dirt, rocks prodding you in all sorts of regions, usually with a sun baking you with 40 degree or more heat, I often thought of the lush green grass we lay on at Papakura, under 20 degrees or so.

Training in the desert – firing at target disks. (Source: Matapihi - http://beta.natlib.govt.nz/records/23235333)

The reality about war's hardships was slowly starting to sink in for my comrades and I. Being a member of the New Zealand Army was not the 'walk in the park' we thought it would be. Discipline, fitness, rules, behaviour, marching, parades, training, sickness, and many other demands and expectations made the reality of what we were experiencing completely different from our initial perceptions of how the war would turn out for us. The Greece and North African campaigns were still to come!

From Training in Egypt to Fighting in Greece–April-1941

On the 13th March, 1941, the NZ Division (2nd Echelon) was deployed to Greece, to assist British and Australian forces in defending the country from invading German forces.

The operation here was devised by British Prime Minister Winstone Churchill and the British Cabinet in response to

pledges made in 1939 to assist Greece if threatened with invasion. On 6th April 1941, New Zealand clashed with the Nazi war machine as Hitler unleashed his unbeaten Air Force and Armoured Divisions into Northern Greece. German superiority in equipment and numbers swiftly overwhelmed the British and Commonwealth Forces. Hitler was concerned that if Greece became a British ally then oilfields in Romania he relied on for fuel would be at risk from Greek attack.
(Source: www.kiwiveterens.co.nz/walking- wounded- only.)

Leaving Port Said, we sailed across the Mediterranean, three troopships in convoy and unescorted. This was a high risk scenario as German twin engine Junkers Ju 88s with their bombs were waiting to strike troopships on the water. On board our ship were just 11 Bren guns, we had no other artillery. Two German bombers attacked the three ships. Had there been an attack from a squadron of fighters the outcome may well have turned out to be very different and this story could have ended here. On this particular occasion things turned out ok, tragedy being avoided as our crew proceeded to shoot a German Junker through the open bomb doors (some eight feet long). The plane was last seen heading away from the ship, a trail of smoke streaming out from behind the tail.

The Anglo Canadian (Source: www.uboat.net)

Arriving at Port Piraeus situated towards the bottom of Greece close to Athens, our NZ Division set up camp near the port. Bren carriers, ammunitions, boxes of grenades and 303 rifles were unloaded. Smith & Weston revolvers were issued to Bren Carrier drivers along with six bullets. Greece had not yet declared war on Germany but did so shortly after Allied troops set up camp here. Because there had not yet been an official declaration of war, the unusual and unexpected sight of German officers, stoically standing by their vehicles plastered with swastikas surprised us all. It all seemed like a stage show.

Entering Piraeus, Greece. (Source: NZETC – Author Henderson, Jim Part of: The Official History of New Zealand in the Second World War 1939–1945.)

Our first day was spent on leave. A popular pastime on leave is to taste the local brews. This is what our bunch of lads did, so much so that we lost all sense of time, easy to do when drowning our sorrows sampling local Mavrodaphne, a powerful Greek red wine. Just for a little variety we experimented with Ouzo, an easy to drink, liquorice flavoured spirit. Having survived the night somehow, our early morning started with a few thick black coffees. Having by now realised the dilemma our unit was in we beat a hasty retreat back to camp. But too late – on our return we found out in horror that our main party had already left. To catch up we had to meet up with the departing train quick smart. Needless to say when our OC caught up with us on the train he let us know how disgusted he felt.

"You call yourselves soldiers, yet you let the drink get the better of you. Let it be known that this behaviour must never occur again. Now get to your positions and ponder on your unacceptable conduct."

We were unanimous in our response. "Yes sir!"

Some of us had got off to a bad start. The train journey was not a pleasant one. Arriving at our destination, we had to take up positions along a new defensive line (the Aliakmon Line north of Mt Olympus), a line formed between Mount Olympus and the Aliakmon River. Being a Sunday, a service was held at which it was announced that Greece had declared war on Germany.

This was the real thing, it was not a practice exercise anymore.

Battle of Vevi (1941) (Also Known as Battle of the Klidi Pass)

Meanwhile, bombing raids were still continuing over parts of Britain. Germany had invaded Yugoslavia and Greece. Having eventually caught the train carrying our troops and artillery up to the front line, the two to three hour journey allowed our nerves to settle a little, but not for too long, as another unknown awaited us.

Upon reaching Mt Olympus it quickly became apparent that without suitable and sufficient firepower and being hugely outnumbered, any front on battle with the German forces would be futile and doomed to fail. This was not the way it was meant to be.

Bren Carrier crews typically consisted of the driver and alongside him the front gunner. In the back would be two or sometimes three bren-gunners.

Also in the back would be a few steel boxes full of hand grenades. The front gun was fixed and fired through a small aperture located in the front panel. The men in the rear operated hand held Bren Guns. On the Bren Carrier crew in Greece, I had been delegated as the driver. My weaponry consisted of a small revolver and six bullets.

I asked the issuing officer "How the heck are one small revolver and six bullets going to protect me in a mass invasion?"

"You need to do the best you can," came the reply. That answer left me none the wiser.

One might well wonder how a revolver would help me against an advancing army! The end tips of bullets were sometimes cut flat.

This would increase the likelihood of inflicting fatal wounds on the enemy, thereby stopping them in their tracks. However, this was an illegal practice and certainly not condoned.

Bren gun carriers on the road in Greece, 21 April 1941 (Source: Imperial War Museum Collection. The British Army in Greece 1941© IWM (E 2524))

In my crew operating the fixed Bren Gun beside me, was John Best. John, a very capable sportsman, had played six matches for the All Blacks. Contact with John was lost after the Greek campaign. One more lost contact to put into the basket of 'wish I knew what happened to?'

2nd NZEF soldiers in their Morris truck during the Greek campaign. (Source: NZ Department of Internal Affairs. Ref: DA-01591-F. Alexander Turnbull Library, Wellington, New Zealand)

With no anti-tank guns and Bren Guns firing 303 bullets which bounced harmlessly off the German tanks, a retreat was ordered almost before any action started. The mixed Australian-British-New Zealand and Greek formation (the Mackay Force) was tasked to halt the German advance. With just 12,000 troops, 4-5,000 Australian, facing the German attacking troops belonging to the 9th Panzer Division and the LSSAH, allied troops were massively outnumbered.

Mt Olympus, Metaxas Line, Aliakmon Line, and retreat to Corinth. (Source: Wotan's Children - 5th Gebirgs Division attacks the Metaxas Line)

Across the water, not too far away in the distance I could see Salonika (Thessalonica) being lit up by heavy bombing. The German 9th Panzer Division broke through at Klidi Pass, (a winding, steep, rocky and treeless pass up to 1000 meters high) having arrived in force and with self-propelled guns they climbed the slopes, thought impossible by those who knew the place. This support, given to their infantry forced the British down the mountain, many taken prisoner. The first New Zealand prisoners fighting as members of our New Zealand unit were taken here as well. I could easily have been one of them. This action effectively sealed our (the Allies') defeat at Vevi.

The Battle of Vevi (also know as the Battle of the Klidi Pass) took place over two days on 11th & 12th April, 1941. Because of the Axis force's superiority our NZ Division began its withdrawal along the eastern seaboard.

My first real experience of being in the heart of battle, although focused almost entirely on retreat, very quickly got me thinking. How was it that our own troops were so outnumbered by the German forces? How was it that the German tanks could over-run the deeply dug trenches as if they simply weren't there?

The strategies of battle became apparent – first bombardment from the air followed up by advancing artillery, tanks and infantry.

In attempting to block the advancement, anything to obstruct the advancing Panzers would be placed in their way – old broken down vehicles, mines, rocks, rubbish etc but the German forces simply overran the barriers with ease. At the same time German airplanes strafed our New Zealand Division positions. A huge tank trap trench was dug by the Greeks (Metaxas Line) but again this was no match for the Germans. Further retreat was made to El E Acman River where another stand was attempted. Our New Zealand troops did well here, supported by capable firepower including 25 pounder artillery and 303 guns. German Stukas with screamers at the front, loaded with two bombs flew over 10 at a time. The screamers blasted out shrieking noise intended to demoralise our New Zealand soldiers. I detested that noise. The German fighter planes would circle and circle and then dive one at a time. No time to picture the scenery! Not many Stukas were hit. Courageous as our men were in making a stand here, the situation quickly became hopeless and the resistance did not last very long. The German Stukas played a large part in driving Allied forces back. Apart from a few Lysanders which were basically artillery spotting planes, the Allied forces offered only token resistance and had nothing to answer the German forces with, particularly in the air.

Going backwards along roads headed back towards Corinth and pressed by the Germans marching forward, a spot covered in green hills and steep gullies was reached. During a short stop here some Bren Carriers and two Humber staff cars were pushed over the precipice. The cars had the oil sump plug removed and after having their engines started, were run dry. It was decided that the staff cars could disappear since the officers whom the cars belonged to had already flown out of Corinth, much to the wonderment of those of us left to do battle. The theory we held onto, being, that the risk of being caught could be reduced by abandoning the vehicles which were of no use to us while retreating and were only slowing us down.

A rest point for troops, Greece. (Source: Ref DA-01603-F. Alexander Turnbull Library, Wellington, New Zealand. httpbeta.natlib.govt.nzrecords22848102)

I came to understand that Churchill's strategy had been to send troops into Greece to confront the Axis troops thus buying extra time for a more important campaign in the Middle East. I worried about that.

The realisation dawned on me that many men had lost their lives in a battle where the enemy so outnumbered our own forces that there could be only one outcome – the loss of soldiers' lives. The excitement I first experienced on boarding the troopship in Wellington was beginning to be dulled by what I saw as the loss of life in an uneven battle. Making sense of war was getting harder. I started asking questions of myself and I began to realise that many more questions were going to be asked. Christmas 1941 in Maadi Camp would see me asking myself one of those questions. The fervour and patriotism I felt when enlisting was slowly but surely being replaced by me trying to now figure out the justifications for war. I mention this again later.

Further retreat was made southwards towards the Corinth Channel where the 4th Brigade were situated holding defensive positions.

During the final stages of the retreat I witnessed a horrific incident which I remember as the 'ambulance incident'. Retreating soldiers, scattered and somewhat disorganised, were being attacked on the ground and from the air. Amongst a grove of olive trees, with shooting happening all around, the uppermost thing in the minds of the men was trying to find ways of escaping the predicament they were in. In amongst the panic and pandemonium an ambulance was seen waiting a few hundred yards away.

I heard some of the men yell out, "Let's make a dash for the ambulance."

For some reason I hesitated and deciding not to go, shouting, " You go, I'll take my chances here."

It was one of those split second decisions you have to make. 'Something' made me decide not to make a run for the ambulance. What was it? To my dismay I witnessed the ambulance, men inside, being strafed and shot to bits by German Messerschmitt 109 fighter planes. The vision of those 109s distinguished by white circles painted on the middle of the propeller and also by the square shaped edges on their wingtips has stayed with me forever. They were instruments of death.

This incident had a dramatic impact on me and I have remembered it all my life. Shaken after witnessing this tragedy, I kept on moving in and out of the trees, diving into ditches or trenches as the 109s buzzed overhead. I remember my two tins of 'bully beef' bouncing around in my heavy great coat (NZ made, superior to the British model which were hairy things not as smooth as the NZ coats). Conditions were icy and cold, wearing coats a necessity. It is no wonder to me that in experiencing such dramatic events, that otherwise such insignificant things as the white circles in the middle of the propeller blades and tins of bully beef bouncing around in heavy coats would probably have been long forgotten.

German dive-bomber shot down by the Divisional Cavalry during the withdrawal in Greece. (Source: NZETC – Author: Loughnan, R. J. M.)

Still retreating, I came across a Maori soldier lying prostrate on the ground, bleeding badly in one leg. I saw his predicament and asked, "How did this happen?" even though I knew the answer.

He looked at me muttering something like, "we need to stop the bleeding."

Recalling the lessons taught to us in our military training I took a tourniquet from a pocket kit and applied it to the seriously wounded soldier's leg. Next I picked him up, 20 stone and all and put him on a Ute type truck driven by An English gentleman.

I yelled at the driver, "Please take this guy straight to the field hospital." The driver seemed to understand and asked, "Are you coming too?"

I jumped in and accompanied the wounded man for a little while as we headed towards Corinth, then jumped off when the driver diverted to the field hospital.

"Look after him," I yelled.

His name was Win Panahoe. I met him some 10 years later working at the Auckland wharfs. I recognized Win but not being entirely sure if it was the same man I had assisted in Greece I asked, "Can I see your leg?"

Win, surprised why someone out of the blue wanted him to roll up his trousers to see his leg looked at me quizzically, "What for?"

I replied "I may be the person who picked you up and saved your life over in Greece."

"That's it," he said.

"That's it," I said.

Win pulled up his trouser leg and showed me his scars of battle. We had an immediate mutual respect for each other, however, we did not really develop a deeper friendship, preferring to just acknowledge each other in passing and not wanting to glorify what happened between us a decade previously.

I recall another episode on the wharfs when Win pointed out crates of whiskey being unloaded from a ship across the way and saying "I have some of that."

"What do you mean, you have some of that?"

"If you want some, I can get it for you," Win said.

"I'm not so keen on whiskey," was my response, trying to deflect any possibility of ending up with stolen goods. Truth is, I actually didn't mind a drop of that stuff.

This conversation occurred when Win was working on the winch of the ship we were unloading. When crates broke open while unloading, many wharfies considered any 'acquisition' of the contents to constitute a trade 'perk'. Not every wharfie did however, and with my conservative nature and not being one to take risks I kindly refused any offer to take some of it for myself. Anyway I believed I could easily have been caught at the wharf gates by the customs guards. So I never did receive any 'free' whiskey.

I don't know what happened to Win in the subsequent years but I do know that Win's brother, who was a spitting image of Win, also worked on the wharfs some years after I met Win there.

Back to the retreat in Greece, disorganised soldiers found conditions testing. The coldness, snow and wearing of thick army coats in the Greek terrain are things you just don't forget. Having withdrawn all the way back down the 320 kilometres of the eastern seaboard, we began preparations to board ships for transport back to Egypt and Maadi, although we would first be stationed at Crete for a few days.

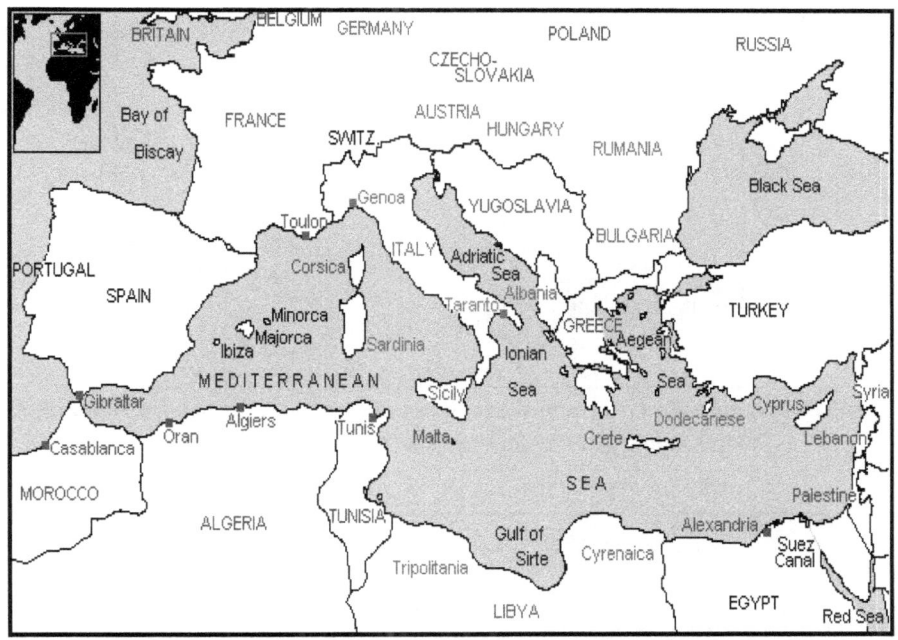

Mediterranean map - Greece to Egypt. (Source: www. Naval-History.Net - Gordon Smith Campaign and Battle Maps of World Wars I and II, and the Falklands War)

To Crete, Back to Egypt Again and to Sidi Bishr, May 1941

At Corinth troop ships were preparing to sail for Crete. At the port I could see only one troopship guarded by Scottish guards acting as army wardens. I heard an order directed my way, "Soldier, this is an embarking point and you must stay under cover tonight and await further instructions in the morning"

I acknowledged the guard's order with, "I shall do that".

I hesitated for a moment, then disregarded the instruction and headed for the nearest ship anyway. The first 600 soldiers got on board, any others had to find the next ship. The sailing was scheduled for 3 am. The ship we found ourselves on was the HMS Isis D87, a British ship attached to a flotilla evacuating troops from Greece. *(Record shows in May 1941: Deployed in blockade of Cape Bon area to intercept craft evacuating Axis forces from North Africa Operation Retribution – (Source: naval-history.net).* The darkness of the early hour offered some protection against possible German air attacks. I felt a little better about that.

HMS destroyer Isis – Corinth to Crete. (Source: www u-boat.net - Gudmundur Helgason. Also see service record a naval-history.net)

Evacuating Greece. (Source: www.militaryphotos.net-g67greece8)

The journey across the Mediterranean from Corinth to Crete took four to five hours. Landing at Suda Bay, the hungry amongst us were fed sandwiches and buns. The last thing I wanted to see for a while was 'bully beef'. I had had enough of that for the time being.

The evacuation of troops from Greece occurred over 22nd-29th April. We left Greece on 28th April, 1941.

Arrival In Crete

Arriving in Crete, we were uncertain as to what the plans would be for us. It eventuated that evacuating troops from Greece would be split between those staying at Crete and those to be posted on to Egypt. After a couple of days I learnt I would be moving on to Egypt.

Had I stayed to face the Germans in Crete, the outcome may well have been quite different for me.

A few weeks later, on May 20th, the Germans attacked the three main Crete airfields with a mass of paratroopers and gliders, the first such invasion of the war. After seven days of fighting the Allied forces were again outnumbered and the battle of Crete was lost. By June 1st, 1941, the Allied forces were evacuated from Crete. The Germans suffered losses of more than 4000 dead, many of these paratroopers, as well as 370 aircraft destroyed. The Allies suffered nearly 4000 killed plus the loss of nine Royal Navy ships sunk. *(Note: As with many such battles, some authorities dispute the actual number of casualties.)*

Told that we were to move on to Egypt we waited while arrangements were made. I wondered what type of ship I was to embark on next. Experiences revealed to me that it was just as dangerous on board ship as it was with feet on the ground.

Second NZEF awaiting evacuation from Crete. (**Source : Alexander Turnbull Library. Ref:DA-01040)**

Second NZEF resting in a village street in Crete awaiting evacuation from Crete. (Source : Alexander Turnbull Library. Ref:DA-01157-F)

Once on board the ship, there was standing room only. The plan was for the destroyers to transport soldiers out to the middle of the harbour to waiting cargo ships acting as troop carriers, ready to take troops across to Egypt. Reaching the transfer point in the harbour, our group was allocated to the Thurland Castle which could carry a complement of 1000 soldiers.

Thurland Castle (Source: Alexander Turnbull Library – Photographer – P V Graves. Ref. DA-07137-G)

Getting on board safely, proving to be a feat in itself. Climbing up the rope ladders slung over the ship's side, tested us all. On board, only deck space was available, 1000 soldiers on the same deck, side by side with little room to move. Once under sail I saw flashes lighting up the sky from battles raging three or four kilometres up the harbour. A feeling of being 'protected' a second time came over me as I realised that, had we been seen by German fighters roaming the skies we would have been simple targets or 'goners' as they say. All we could do was lay on deck, defenceless at the mercy of German air power, should we have been seen. Reaching Egypt from Crete just couldn't come quick enough!

Sidi Bishr

Once again finding ourselves down to skin and bone, our troops were sent by truck (a five hour trip) from Alexandria up to a navel rehabilitation base at Sidi Bishr. Sidi Bishr was to act as home for two to three months. Needing rest and recuperation after our experiences in Greece, ample supplies of rum, beer and cigarettes were provided to help our recovery. More I think to divert our minds off war rather than to build up our bodies.

The expansive white sandy beaches bordering the clear blue Mediterranean Sea stretching out to the horizon was picture postcard stuff to us, the water calling us soldiers worn out by enemy engagement. Bathing in the cool water was a blessing but in the sea there lurked danger - the giant Mediterranean clam best described as an overgrown oyster. Putting a foot on one of these risked severe injuries as the clam would slowly close its jaws around your enclosed foot. It paid to be wary.

CZ military camp Sidi Bishr (near Alexandria), Egypt 1940. (Source: 'Sahara' = cz-camp 004 Sidi Bish)

Being a rest camp, training for war took a backseat for a while. Apart from the ever available alcoholic beverages and swimming, 'two-up' gambling games provided another entertainment option. Organised by the Australian contingent, this form of entertainment was guaranteed to be supported with exuberance and eager anticipation, common amongst those of us participating in gambling pursuits. There was nothing too complicated about playing '2-up'. A circle drawn in the sand, two coins, a 'spinner' and the banker controlled the game. The two coins were tossed (spun) into the air. Cries of expectation, many urging encouragement for two heads rang out as the metal pieces spun through the air, all eyes fixated on the coins as they landed in the circle. Two heads and you doubled your money.

Some circles of social comment around the camp suggested that the Australians tended to be more standoffish (I thought so anyway) whereas Kiwis were friendlier. The German General Rommel was known to favour our New Zealand soldiers as he thought them more stubborn. The British could be snobbish, snooty. This was a comment I had read in the Army Gazette, provided monthly at Maadi camp. The Gazette consisted of only a few pages but it provided welcome reading to soldiers eager for news – any news.

Another form of communication I remember was all the propaganda stuff. My fellow soldiers talked about this many a time and our superiors often reiterated warnings such as "watch out for propaganda as it is only aimed at 'unsettling' you. The enemy will try and cause confusion in your mind".

However we were not told that our side did much the same. We came to discover that in England, Greece and in Egypt; posters, radio broadcasts, newspapers, pamphlets, any sort of propaganda was used as a medium to try to rattle our troops. Posters were stuck on walls, fences and buildings.

A 'Don't talk' propaganda poster. (Source: American WW2 propaganda Posters. National War Museum. Artist: Glenn Grothe & Koehler Ancona)

A favourite spot used by those displaying propaganda materials was on the walls of many English pubs, posters urging the like of "Don't talk – walls have ears – the enemy is listening!"

It was difficult to pretend that all these 'messages' had no effect on soldiers as they seemed to reside in the back of my mind and I still recall many of them today.

Two more propaganda posters on display in England. (Source: American WW2 propaganda Posters. National War Museum)

I can recall seeing thousands of leaflets scattered around on the desert floor, dropped there by German aircraft. The message asking New Zealand soldiers why were they fighting England's war and telling them they must go home. The leaflets were signed 'Adolf Hitler'. In Sidi Bishr, mess room and canteen radios tuned into German stations heard Lord Haw Haw broadcast exhortations such as, "We are going to blow you up" and "New Zealanders, you don't belong here; this is not your war, go home". At first I did not know who Lord Haw Haw was, he sounded quite convincing with his own peculiar English accent.

Lord Haw Haw was the nickname given to several announcers on the English language propaganda radio programme 'Germany calling' broadcast by Nazi German radio to audiences in Great Britain. The programs started on the 18th September and went on until 30th April 1945. William Joyce, born in America became the best recognised Lord Haw Haw. His distinctive pronunciation and typical introduction of "Jairmany calling, Jairmany calling," well remembered. Joyce was captured by British forces at the end of the war. He was eventually hanged for treason on January 3rd, 1946.
Source: en.wikipedia.org/wiki/Lord_ Haw-Haw

The English in turn dropped thousands of propaganda pamphlets over Germany.

Sidi Bishr provided us with a welcome relief from the excursions in Greece and gave us valuable rest and recovery time.

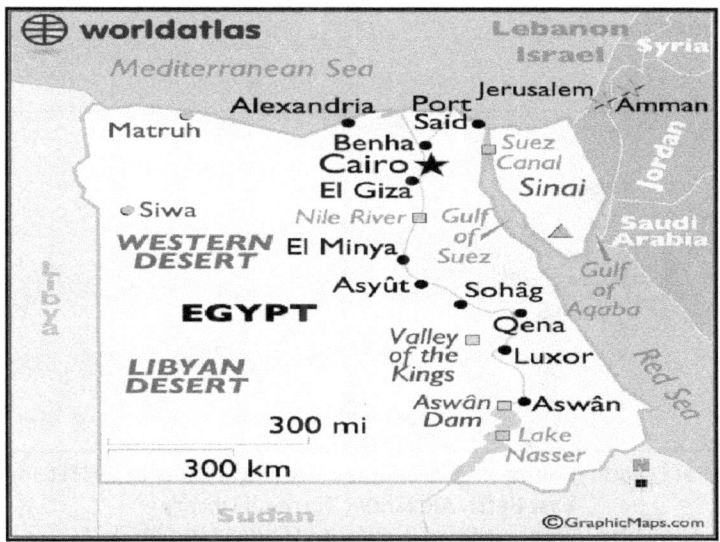

Sidi Bishr -Alexandria – Egypt – rest and recovery camps. (Source: About.com Africa Travel)

Maadi Again

All good things come to an end and after three months of this better life at rest camp it was back to business and a return to Maadi. More marches of 14 miles, into the desert and into 40-plus degrees centigrade. We all had to survive; sunburn, dysentery, flies, scorpions, hot days and cold nights. A few more months of preparation and training had to be endured before the next posting. War had really only just begun.

Apart from regular route marches out into the desert, parades were also common practice. These took place more as a discipline measure or to present to officers, especially visiting officers. Parades were not as demanding as the route marches but still trying under desert conditions. There we would be, attempting to stand at attention, gazing directly ahead of us as flies bit and crawled around our faces, testing our extreme urges to swat them away. One of the bigger parades held at Maadi happened during a visit from Winston Churchill, shortly after the Greece campaign. On display were the Maori Battalion and our Divisional Cavalry along with troops and Bren Carriers. When important dignitaries such as he came to visit there was no mucking around, parading was very prim and proper, you behaved or else!

Parades at Maadi. (Sources: J B McKinney – Medical Units of 2 NZEF in Middle East (left). Alexander Turnbull Library - http://mp.natlib.govt.nz/detail/?id=33194 (Right))

Route marches and parades were much tougher than the training marches and parades in Papakura or in Aldershot. Conditions in the Western Desert varied markedly from those found in deserts such as the Sahara. In Egypt the so called desert sand was not actually sand, but dirt. Dust infiltrated everything, boots, shorts, shirts, food and weapons. Dust clouds rose up as soon as anything moved on the ground, boots or vehicles. Rocks were far more common than in sandy deserts. Should rain fall, conditions would become muddy with lots of 'stick'. I can't say that I loved all of this!

The note in the Event Book on the next page records a soldier's feelings about Egypt.

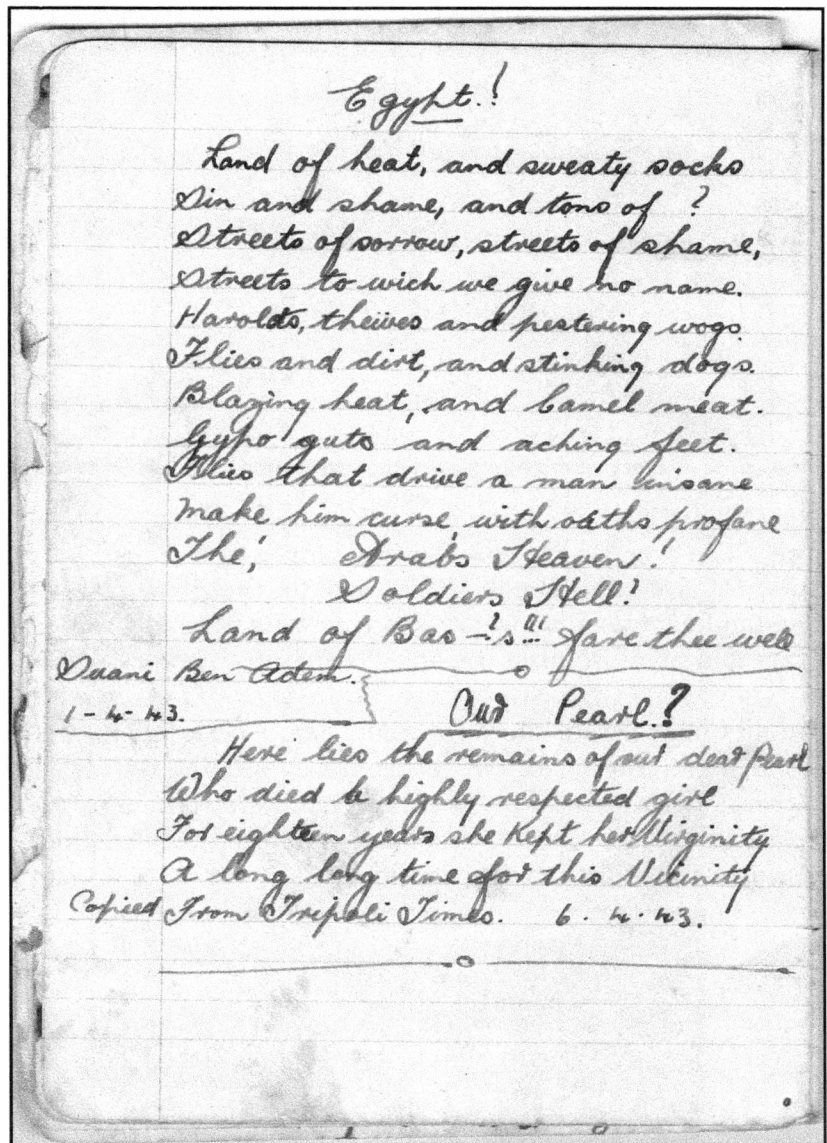

Egypt! Land of heat and sweaty socks.

Training in the desert - a moment's respite. Pop second from left, in the middle row.

I recall an exercise where we were deployed to an area a few miles south of Cairo and Maadi. This was to the Tura Caves. Our understanding was that we were there on a training exercise to prepare and organise for a possible German paratroops' invasion. I learnt later that the caves were destined to carry reserves of ammunition. We were there for about two weeks, sleeping in the caves at night. The history of the Tura Caves is interesting in that these were not a natural phenomenon but were formed by ancient Egyptians who used the area as a quarry to form the huge limestone blocks used in building their pyramids.

The Tura Caves – two weeks training – a connection to the ancient Pyramids (Source: Alexander Turnbull Library. Ref. DA-04264-F. Photographer – G.F.Kaye)

> **GOOD-BYE TO OLD NEW ZEALAND**
>
> Good-bye to old New Zealand
> For we are off to a far distant land
> Good bye to all our sweethearts
> For we'll be gone along long time
> To fight to fight for freedom
> For the land that gave us birth
> And we'll never forget New Zealand
> The sweetest little spot on earth.
>
> Anti Paratroops - July 1942 - Tura Caves (Maadi area)

Thoughts turn to New Zealand in this note written at Tura Caves.

At Maadi, meal time consisted of good old 'bully beef' or sometimes South African beef or even camel meat served with Egyptian-type potatoes along with a local 'green'. The camel meat was thin and chewable but definitely not the same as the New Zealand beef I ate at home. Our troops lined up at the cookhouse with their Dixie dishes (small 2 x 8 inch aluminium pots) returning to our tents to eat. Christmas was treat time, offering Christmas fruit cake and a pour of custard over the top. The meal was enjoyed by us all and a welcome relief after the monotony of consuming regular helpings of bully beef out in the field.

Mail day happened once or twice a month. It was always a special day but especially at Christmas time as the promise of eagerly awaited treats saw the men rush to the mail dump.

Christmas mail at the Maadi Camp Post office, December 1942. (Source: National Library of NZ - http://mp.natlib.govt.nz/detail/?id=4865 – Maxwell Stuart Carrie)

I remember one particular Christmas mail delivery when I found my own special treat waiting for me in a tin. My dad Charles not only sent me a big fat fruit cake but also went to the trouble of putting the cake in a tin and then solder the lid all the way around. Of course this required a marathon effort at the camp to remove the lid.

Advice was free " Charlie, open that thing, I can smell the cake from here" and "Give it to me, I'll get the flaming lid off."

With eager anticipation and lots of effort and passing around the tin (like pass the parcel) the lid eventually came off, removed by someone, somehow. With the cake no longer intact, the ready made pieces presented themselves to be eaten. Did I get the first piece? Not likely! The fact that dad Charles had gone to a great deal of trouble to ensure I received my Christmas treat showed the thoughts he obviously had for me. He didn't know it but his popularity status rose amongst my mates, as mine did!

"Thanks for the cake Charlie."

The North African Campaign
Operation Crusader – 2nd NZ Division, Western Desert, September to November, 1941.

To help understand how and when Pop fitted into the numerous movements and battles which occurred during fighting in Egypt a few short summaries have been researched and included here to support Pop's own recollections. There were many battles, forays, advances and retreats. Many were intense, yet for the most part 'time' was spent in training camp, at rest camp or sometimes moving great distances to new strategic positions. In some of the well documented battles Pop's involvement was not always at the front line remembering also that his role as a Bren Carrier driver was to support and guide mostly infantry troops.

Researched references and quotes are identified, typed in italics.

Summary – Background – The North African Campaign – NZHistory.net.nz, New Zealand history online

The main fighting element of 2NZEF was the 16,000-strong 2nd New Zealand Division. 'The Div' was commanded by First World War Victoria Cross (VC) winner Major-General Bernard 'Tiny' Freyberg. After returning to Egypt following the disastrous campaigns in Greece and Crete, the New Zealand Division entered the fray in North Africa during Operation Crusader in November 1941. For the next year, they saw action in the Western part of Egypt, with several forays into Libya.
The New Zealanders saw little action during the initial stages of the North African campaign. Most of the fighting took place between the Western Desert Force (composed of British, Indian and Australian troops) and Italian forces. British and Commonwealth troops did not think much of their 'Itie' opponents. Some units fought well, but in general the Italians were badly equipped and poorly led. Many Italian troops were ambivalent about fighting on the German side and

unwilling to give their lives for a cause in which they did not believe.

With Allied attention focused on Greece, General Field Marshal Erwin Rommel transformed the situation in Africa. Driving east, he forced the Allies back into Egypt, leaving an Australian Division besieged in the Libyan port of Tobruk. After two unsuccessful attempts to relieve Tobruk, General Claude Auchinleck, C-in-C Middle East, decided to launch Operation Crusader – a large-scale infantry and armoured offensive designed to crush the Africa Corps and lift the siege. This operation would provide the setting for the New Zealand first foray into the desert.

Short Timelines

September 12 1941 – 2nd NZ Division moved to Baggush in the Western Desert

November 11 1941 – 2nd NZ Division moves from Baggush to assembly point near Matruh Siwa. First time all of NZ forces are together.

November 18 1941 – Tank battle between 8th Army and Axis begins south and south-east of Tobruk

November 26, 1941 – 2nd NZ Division links with garrison at Tobruk, NZ troops (4th Brigade) capture Belhamed and (6th Brigade) Sidi Rezeg

November 27-30, 1941 – Axis army returns to Tobruk front. Overruns several NZ held points, taking many prisoners of war.

(Source - Operation Crusader; the North African Campaign / NZHistory.net.nz, New Zealand history online)

My Recollections

While the Germans were clashing with the British further south, the NZ 5th Brigade and Divisional Cavalry (my unit) were tasked with advancing on Sollum, having earlier crossed the Libyan border into Cyrenaica and overrunning the Italians defending this position. Meanwhile the 4th Brigade were asked to advance on Bardia and the 6th Brigade on Sidi Rezeg, an isolated spot at 'nowhere' in the desert. As bad luck would have it, while these advances were happening, Rommel was falling back after unsuccessful attempts to relieve Axis units around the Libya / Egypt border. Rommel ran straight through our New Zealand lines in the south west, overrunning the 5th Brigade. Several New Zealand battalions suffered heavy casualties as German tanks swept over the escarpments at Sidi Rezeg and Belhamed. Thousands of our New Zealanders were taken prisoner and sent to POW camps in Italy.

German tank burning in the desert. (Source : Wikipedia – free encyclopaedia)

Italian tanks moving across the desert. (Source: Wikipedia – free encyclopaedia – Fiat M13/40 tanks – WW2)

The distances we travelled while moving around the desert and from base camp (Maadi) to various action points could involve thousands of kilometres. Such was the case in this battle. It was a long way from Maadi across Egypt, to cross the border into Libya.

I spent many a night under desert stars. Night skies openly displayed their beauty to my gazing eyes below. Many soldiers would have sent thoughts homeward on a star but for me the longing to get back home to Shaddock Street did not figure so much since I still had unresolved issues about leaving home. I just didn't ponder over such thoughts as much as others possibly did. However, I did begin to realise how different my experiences were to what I thought they might be when enlisting in Whangarei. There was plenty of time to think lying under the stars. Anticipation and anxieties about the following day's uncertainties kept churning around thoughts in my mind. There was no manual about how to deal with these thoughts. You had to deal with them as best as you could. I was in a permanent situation, until when I did not know? Anything voluntary about being here had disappeared soon after the enlistment process. You couldn't just pack up and go home.

> **My Dug-Out** *Mersa Matruh area*
> *Sidi Haneish*
>
> There's a place in my heart which no Jerry can own,
> It's my own little dug-out, my own home sweet home.
> Sure I love the dear rafters that fall on my head,
> And the fleas that infest my dirty old bed.
> My dear little dugout so close to the sea,
> Oh, God bless you, and cleanse you, and keep you, for me.
>
> *Parade* (sung to the tune of Mother of Mine)

From my 'Events Book'. Note mention of Mersa Matruh and Sidi Haneish; desert spots I'd seen.

Troops slept with their boots on in the desert. The nights in the sands are cold. Within minutes of sunset it became dark and often little chilly winds would whisper across the sand. In making a bed for the night, I would excavate a little sand, easier to do than making a motel bed. A minute or two and it was done. On most occasions I would not have to excavate too far down before a few rocks appeared. It is common for rocks to be found scattered throughout the desert, however they are more prominent closer to coastal areas which is where we generally were. Many rocks had scorpions under them. Big black beetles set up house in any dung lying around on the desert floor. I scored a few scorpion stings, once when one hid in my boots. Even after shaking my boots, which was a recommended practice, this fella hung in there refusing to come out and stung the first feet that entered – mine!

"Get out of here, you bugger," I exclaimed, in pain.

Then there were tarantula spiders occupying spaces the nasties didn't. Not nice things to find, but the desert did belong to them. There were those not too concerned with leaving nature be, and who saw fun in pitting one creature against another. To them it was a 'sport' of sorts, a game played in the desert. Those so inclined to play the game would make a ring of fire in the sand using petrol, and inside the ring place two tarantulas and three or four scorpions. Left to do battle, the tarantulas would usually come out on top. I make no secret of the fact that I just didn't like those creatures. Whether boiling billies out in remote desert spots or back at camp, if I saw any I would do away with them – self protection of course! These actions of mine did not go unnoticed by my fellow soldiers. I quickly earned the nickname of 'Killer Knill'

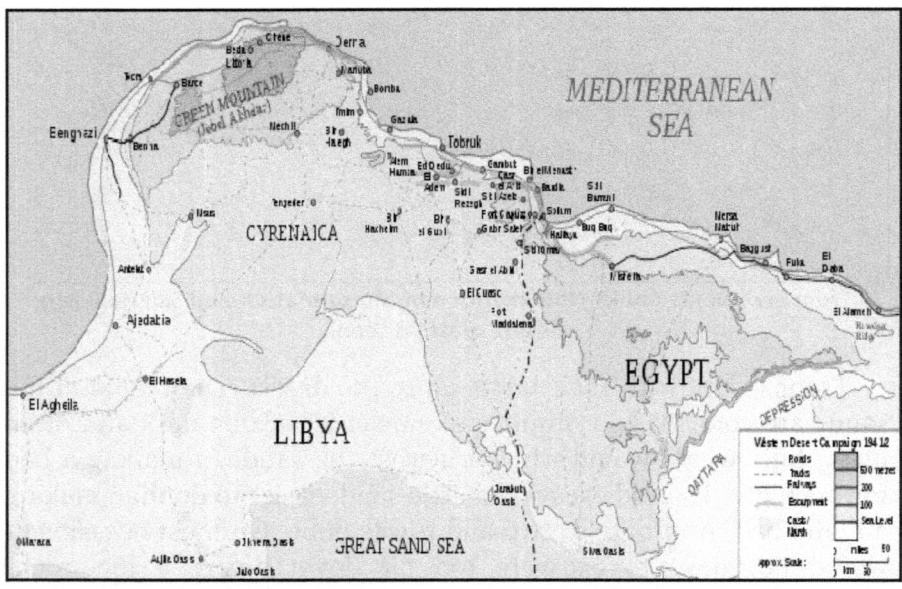

Map showing Libya and Egypt – giving an idea of the rather vast distances which were travelled during various battles. (Source: Wikipedia – Western Desert Battle Area 1941 en.svg. Steven Kirrage)

The NZ 2nd Echelon assembled at Baggush on 26th November 1941– the first time all 20,000 of us had gathered together. Here preparations started for the eminent El Alamein campaign. This was a time for organising our troops, equipment and air forces.

My Life – the Meanderings of Pop Knill

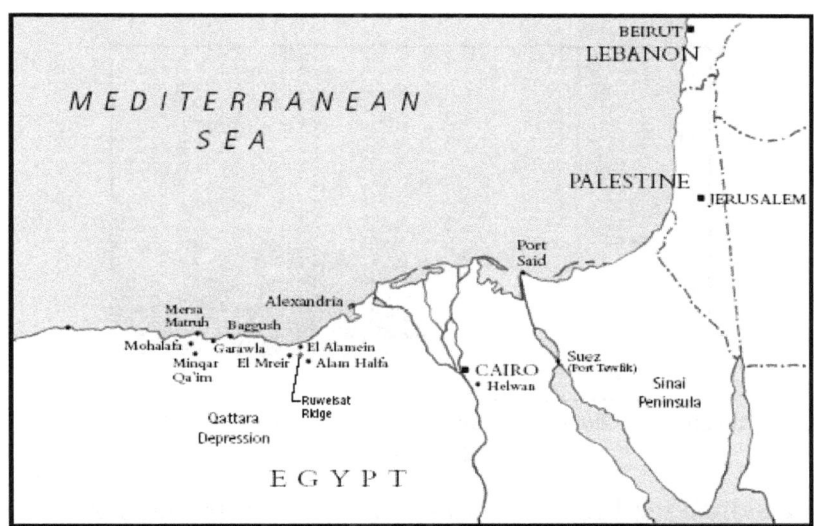

Map indicating the ports and rest/recovery areas and El Alamein. (Source: Politic.ie – drico #80 – nthafrica – 005 – btn)

Push to Sollum, Bardia and Sidi Rezeg - November 1941
My recollections…

Sidi Rezeg was a strategic location, not a town, just a place in the open. The British air force notified 5th Brigade Army command under Brigadier Hargest that a large contingent of 3,000 or 4,000 Axis troops supported by heavy tanks was approaching. Having been given this information, concerns were raised since the NZ Army lacked tanks. Aware of the situation, a divisional officer decided to take a company of 40 or so men, of which I happened to be one, and move some 25 miles north taking with us a NZ Army artillery 25 pounder gun. Arriving at Monastery Escarpment – a place with just a few caves in the desert, we took up our positions (this spot is not well documented in WW2 articles). The divisional officer leading our small unit made the decisions. We had no radio. Our unit took cover in the caves. Up the valley came a small German unit. Having seen one or two of our lads near the caves the Germans fired a few rifle shots our way. The German force consisted of five trucks filled with German infantry soldiers with rifles. Our 25 pounder gun was loaded and fired, blowing away two or three of the enemy trucks. That was enough for the Germans and they fled. We had won this little battle.

Rolling through the dust of the desert. (Source: Dust in the desert – NZETC – WH2diCaPO17b(h280))

At Sidi Rezeg high casualties were suffered by our NZ Division during heavy fighting which included hand-to-hand combat with bayonets, something the Germans did not like and I would think not really liked by New Zealanders fighting there either.

Operation Crusader consisted of lots of forays and battles, intense battles but mostly short and sharp in duration. Often we did not really know we were in the desert. Confusion being something shared by many soldiers.

In the aftermath of Crusader, the New Zealanders licked their wounds back in Egypt. With 879 dead, 1700 wounded and over 2000 prisoners taken, the New Zealander Division had fought its most costly battle of the war.

(Source: From-Operation Crusader; the North African Campaign / NZHistory.net.nz, New Zealand history online)

Return to Maadi and Alexandria - Nov/Dec 1941

Having been battered by the Axis forces in the Crusader campaign the opportunity of a return to Maadi was a blessing. There would be a significant time period before the big battle of El Alamein was to begin. Back at camp we experienced further reorganisation, more training and also time for rest and relaxation in Alexandria.

The battle at El Alamein and the push through to Tripoli would be my final involvement in the war.

Spare time at camp presented plenty of opportunities for reflection. More reflections for me, once again searching to find justifications for war, and answers I could believe in. I struggled more and more but I couldn't really find any justification. How could all this fighting and killing be justified and what purpose did it serve? These were the questions I was asking myself, why was I here and for what purpose? I questioned why war stopped for three days at Christmas and then started again. Increasingly, I wondered to myself, 'If they could do this for Christmas then why couldn't they stop forever?' Were the political justifications for war based on fighting for freedom and democracy for the masses or more to do with satisfying personal ideologies or were they a struggle for power? Who made the decisions in war? Answers didn't come to me, not many anyway. Freedom of expression was being fought for, but in the theatre of war, I felt no room was allowed for voices that might question the decision makers.

In my unit, some saw me as a rebel who sometimes asked out loud "Why if war could be stopped for three days at Christmas, couldn't it be stopped permanently?"

Mates would take me aside and quietly advise me, "Charlie, you need to keep your mouth shut, don't say out loud what you feel privately or you will risk being court-martialled."

I understood that, however questioning how things were was natural for me. I still found myself feeling proud fighting for my country, it was all part of the struggle. Then I thought of how I so willingly volunteered way back in Maungaturoto, I thought of why so many did not come with us. The feelings we soldiers had is illustrated well by the poem on the next page taken from the Events Book. *(Note how the poem is in two parts and appears to be written in different hands, by different soldiers.)*

My Friends Who Stayed at Home

I'm pulling down my colours, I'll
    sling away my web,
I am going down to Cairo to buy my-
    self a bed,
I'm tired of being a soldier, so help
    me bob I am,
Of getting bully and biscuits and of
    eating bread and jam,
Of fighting dirty dagoes and Jerries
    on my own,
When I think of dear old New Zealand
    and my friends who stayed at home.

I'll bet they're walking down the street,
    their cheeks puffed out with pride,
And skiting to their cobbers, how I saved
    their worthless hide,
While here's me in the desert, afraid to show
    my head
For fear some dirty dagoe will fill it
    full of lead.
I am just a nerve-racked soldier — a
    heap of skin and bone,
But still I'll do the fighting, for my
    friends who stayed at home.

When I told my dear old dad that
    I'd volunteered to fight
He said: "God bless you, son, and bring
    you back alright;"
They called us chocolate soldiers
    and five bob tourists too
They said, "You'll never see the front
    or even get a view."

P.T.O.

Poem in Events Book: My Friends Who Stayed at Home.

Getting your laundry done by contracted local labour carried a fairly high risk that you might not get your garments back or that you might well get someone else's. (Source: National Library of NZ - Laundry and local workers, Maadi military camp, Egypt, during World War II. Shows washing bench. Photographer unidentified - http://mp.natlib.govt.nz/detail/?id=75474)

Once more it was back to camp routines, training, route marching, bully beef meals and canteen discussions. There were excursions to Alexandria, travelling there by truck or train. Alexandria was a place more akin to towns of New Zealand with its gardens, beer halls, plants, trees and beaches. Noise accompanied the hustle and bustle of the place but compared to that of screaming dive bombers and pounding artillery it was like soft music. Even the wail from mosque loud speakers calling adherents to prayer became bearable. Not that the place was free of crime or free from those looking to benefit from some illegal activity. No one, including myself was immune from being pick-pocketed or challenged to a fight.

Alexandria and waterfront view. (Source – SSGT Don Kenny Photo Album)

A few mean tricks were played on local citizens. Soldiers on leave often visited Cairo or Alexandria. Travelling in trucks along streets shared with local 'wogs' pulling hand carts, or donkey carts, bringing watermelons to market, a soldier would lean over the side of the truck and with his bayonet stab a watermelon. Not seen as a particularly kind act, the local watermelon man would send abuse and slander in the direction of the disappearing truck, his watermelon gone forever. I wasn't part of that!

A pet – even in the desert – probably at Maadi or on leave, Cairo or Alexandria

Esbikiha Gardens – Sidi Bishr – Alexandria – I met this man on the street and was asked for a cigarette. A security person questioned me asking if I had given this person military secrets. The hat the man is wearing is a 'Fez' hat.

Apart from the usual training exercises, we were occasionally employed on 'war tasks'. One of those tasks included making mines to be used on the battlefield – a high risk occupation. Our 'factory' was located in a brick building on the outskirts of Cairo. The long building was partitioned at intervals by thick brick walls. During my time there we manufactured mines in preparation for the looming battle of El Alamein. Basically, the mines were made using five sticks of gelignite inserted in a 400mm diameter tin housing. The operation was overseen by an army engineer, said to be an expert in mining. I hoped and trusted he was an expert! As fast as the mines were made, they would be bussed out each day by the hundreds, loaded on to trucks destined for El Alamein. I would be posted there shortly after.

El Alamein - November 1942

Background

This battle was the turning point in the Western Allied victory. It turned the tide in the North Africa Campaign and ended Axis hopes of occupying Egypt and controlling the Suez Canal thus gaining access to Middle Eastern oilfields. The battle took 12 days from 25th October to 7th November, 1942. Montgomery had spent six weeks building his forces. His Eighth Army consisted of 220,000 men and 1,100 tanks compared to the Axis force of 115,000 men and 559 tanks of the Panzer Africa unit seriously depleted after their failed offensive at Alam el Halfa.

In between the Crusader operation and the start of El Alamein the 2nd NZ Division were deployed (it was actually at the NZ Government's insistence they go there to recover) to Lebanon-Syria in February 1942 then recalled in June when the 8th Army in Libya was defeated. The 2nd NZ Division narrowly escaped destruction with a breakout at Minqar Qaim (they had been surrounded by a ring of German forces blocking the way out)

*With the breakout at Minqar Qaim the NZ Division fell back to the Alamein Line. At Ruweisat Ridge the New Zealanders seized their objectives but unsupported by British armoured units they had to surrender when German tanks appeared.
(Source: From-Operation Crusader; The North African Campaign/NZHistory.net.nz, New Zealand history online.)*

The (2nd) battle of El Alamein can be broken down into 5 phases;

Stage 1 – The Break In - 23rd & 24th October 1942.

Heavy general bombardment to support Allied advancing infantry. Engineers followed infantry men to clear anti- tank mines so as to clear a path for tanks to follow and to get at the rear of the enemy. The Axis laid mines proved difficult to clear.

Stage 2 – The Crumbling – 24th & 25th October 1942.

The 9th Australian (north) was to plan a crumbling operation for that night. South, the 7th Armoured was to try to break through the minefields. At daybreak artillery and Allied desert forces made 1000 sorties to aid the crumbling plan but little progress was made. Tank battles took place. Allied tanks were repulsed. Allied air attacks continued. Progress stalled.

Stage 3 – The Counter - 26th & 28th October 1942

The entire Axis army has fuel for just three days. Rommel was convinced the main assault was to come from the north.

Montgomery thins his front line and creates a reserve to restore momentum. The reserve included the 2nd NZ Division.

Rommel mounted a major counterattack at Snipe. The 239th Anti-Tank Battery and Rifle Brigade destroyed 22 German and 10 Italian tanks. The Germans began to give up this battle.

The action at Snipe was described as;

> *"The desert was quivering with heat. The gun detachments and the platoons squalled in their pits and trenches, the sweat running in rivers down their dust caked faces. There was a terrible stench. The flies swarmed in black clouds over the dead bodies and excreta and tormented the wounded. The place was strewn with burning tanks and carriers, wrecked guns and vehicles, and over all drifted the smoke and the dust from bursting high explosives and from the blast of guns."*
> *(Source: Action at Swipe, episode of the battle of El Alamein. Lucus- Phillips, Alamein Records – Regiment Historian)*

Stage 4 - Operation Supercharge, 2nd November, 1942 – 26/12/2011

This stage began on the 2nd November 1942. The objective was to destroy enemy armour and force the enemy to fight in the open so as to reduce the Axis already depleted petrol stocks and to attack enemy supply lines. The idea was to clear a path through enemy laid mines. The intended path was not cleared, however the objective of finding and destroying enemy tanks was. Tank losses between both sides were about equal. Considering that the Allies had superior tank numbers the effect was far more dramatic on Rommel's overall tank numbers. Gradually enemy tanks were destroyed. Rommel with just 35 tanks now had to again think withdrawal.

Stage 5 – Breakout- 2nd to 7th November, 1942

"Rommel told Hitler he could not offer any effective opposition. However, Hitler told Rommel to hold tight. The Allied plan now was to chase the Axis (Germans and Italians) retreat and the NZ 2nd Division would head west along desert tracks to the escarpment above Fuka, 97 kilometres away. Ahead lay a path to be forged through minefields. The Italians fought valiantly but were let down by retreating German troops who left them to fight a rear guard action. On November 6th the NZ Division advanced toward Sidi Haneish. There were clashes with German Panzers who lost 16 tanks. The Air Force continued to fly in support. On November 7th while chasing the Germans the rain came, mud appeared everywhere halting the chase. The NZ Division headed for Sollum where the 4th Light Armoured Brigade was positioned at the foot of the Halfaya Pass.

Allied units with superior strength in men and equipment, including Sherman tanks and six pounder tank guns backed up by Spitfires in the air, dominated the Axis forces. The overwhelming superiority had a profound effect on morale. Churchill called the victory 'perhaps the beginning of the end'."
(Source – wikipedia.org/wiki/Second_Battle_of_El_Alamein)

My Recollections

From Maadi I went on to fight at El Alamein. At El Alamein the German positions were bombarded initially by heavy artillery and then later from the air by British Spitfires. German firepower responded with Panzer 75mm and 88mm shelling. The ground rumbled under us as both sides exchanged heavy fire. Continuously, for three days and nights the Germans were pounded by our Allied artillery fire followed by Spitfire attacks from the sky. The Germans were asking for reinforcements to be sent from across the Mediterranean as fuel shortages became a real problem. We knew that the situation was beginning to deteriorate for the German and Italian forces.

Line of Bren carriers ready to move in pursuit of Axis forces, Egypt. (Source: Paton, Harold Gear, 1919-2010. - Photograph taken by H Paton. New Zealand. Department of Internal Affairs. War History Branch: Ref: DA-02726-F. Alexander Turnbull Library, Wellington, New Zealand.)

My delegated role was that of a Bren Carrier driver. Each carrier had a crew of four and sometimes five – with me driving, one beside me in front and two at the back. In the front, a Bren gun was fired through a front positioned aperture. In the back, hand held Bren guns were used when situations demanded it. In this campaign the New Zealand 2nd Division along with my Divisional Cavalry unit, 'C' Squadron provided a support role in assisting the 8th Army. Typically in battle the first action would involve an artillery bombardment followed by engineers sent in to clear mines followed by an infantry advance supported by the Bren Carriers. The role our Bren Carriers played was more of a hit and miss one as the length of time we could remain at the battle front was largely determined by our petrol gauges. As petrol ran low our carriers would have to fall back to reach the New Zealand Army Service Corps trucks bringing up petrol stocks and approaching as close as they could to the battle field.

The Bren Carrier

The Bren Carrier and its role in battle were described as follows:

*Initially this vehicle is used mainly for fighting off small infantry units with its machine gun (normally a Mk.2 LMG or an upgraded Vickers Medium Machine Gun), and quickly ferrying infantry units across the battlefield to wherever they're needed. The Bren Carrier is classified as a light vehicle: despite its armour it does receive damage from small fire and certainly from larger guns as well. Therefore, the Bren Carrier is not expected to engage anything but the smallest enemy units. If not used for ferrying, however, it can always be employed for flanking enemy infantry thanks to its superior speed.
(Source: http://companyofheroes.wikia.com/wiki/Bren_Carrier)*

Here I am with Bren gun in hand and Bren Carrier behind me – photo probably at Maadi – training.

On one particular excursion the death of Hellfire Jack happened. High on the hill at Halfaya Pass, a number of Italian soldiers had surrendered with arms raised. Jack stood up in the Bren Carrier to check what was happening when a lone bullet fired from a surrendering soldier struck and killed him. 'Hellfire' was the nickname given to Jack by compatriots of his who enjoyed being around him and who considered him to be full of 'hellfire'. Prior to gaining this nickname he was known as 'two-finger Jack' since he had lost two fingers on one hand. I remember Jack possessing a special character all his own just as his mates remembered him. He was one of us.

While advancing through Halfaya Pass in the Bren Carrier, escorting the Infantry Division of the 8th Army advance, I witnessed another disturbing scene. Another horrific image imprinted on my bank of memories. Beside the road on either side were two Italian soldiers covered in the dust of the desert, bloated bodies left isolated and alone, never to return home, human, just as the enemy passing them by were human. To me they seemed like dead rabbits lying flat on their backs, left there unburied, dust their only cover. Death staring me in the face as it had done before, death so obvious. Death which seemed such a needless waste, for causes extolled by some and meaningless for others. Scenes seen by many a soldier, contemplated and questioned for lifetimes afterwards. This was the least desired but also the most common scene of war.

My mates pondered death, but I think many were not sure of how to express their feelings about it. One release seemed to be in writing a poem. One in my 'Events Book' expresses such a feeling.

> R.I.P. C/o. Bert – Bill. and Cec. Libyan Desert.
>
> Though the tears in my eyes do not glitter,
> And my face at times does not seem sad,
> There is always that sad longing
> For my cobbers that once I had.

The minefields laid by retreating German forces were particularly dangerous places. Lessons from training told us to watch for mines laid one under another, the intention being that the underneath mine would strike at any unsuspecting engineer or soldier removing the top mine but not aware of the second lying underneath. Another type - spring loaded mines laid just under the surface of the desert floor were designed to explode as infantry marched over them. These mines would be set off with minimal pressure and spring upwards causing severe injury to a soldier's lower limbs. Another common mine clearing method was the use of tanks with 'thrashers'- overgrown scoops.

While the lack of air and artillery support caused many a problem in earlier action around Operation Crusader and as it did before that in Greece, the superiority gained from the extra number of these at El Alamein contributed significantly to the Allied victory. The Spitfires and Hurricanes were brought across from England in cargo ships and railed to air bases in Egypt. This Allied air power and artillery backed up by our Bren Carriers and infantry support was very effective in knocking out any resistance. In reserve to our C Squadron were the A and B Squadrons. As our units dropped back to refuel, the reserve squadrons would take up the charge.

Care had to be taken in the many miles travelled chasing retreating Axis forces, as pockets of German/Italian resistance could spring up anywhere. The wide expanses of the desert offered more places to hide than you might think.

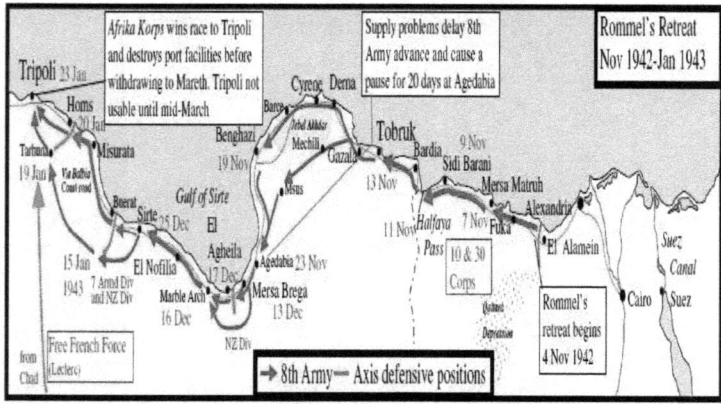

Map showing Axis troops retreat and Allied advance Nov 1942 – Jan 1943

After the Halfaya skirmishes, while still chasing the Axis troops, I received a posting as a driver for a British Intelligence Officer. Travelling the road towards our ultimate destination of Tripoli a collision occurred with a British convey coming the other way. Realising our truck wasn't going anywhere having broken its axle, our crew grouped at the side of the road to figure out what to do. A short time later I heard our Intelligence Officer who had just taken off by foot, yell out, "I'll send a truck back later to come and pick you blokes up."

"Yes sir," we agreed, but were left secretly wondering what the heck he had planned.

It didn't happen, we were left there. Meanwhile, the remaining three of us, noticing a band of Senussi, dug a mound beside the road. We believed that the roving nomad Senussi possibly posed a threat to us since we supposed they may have carried with them a few guns and may have had an unfriendly attitude towards any foreign soldiers occupying their land. The fake grave we dug did not scare off the Senussi as we had intended and rather than being a hostile lot they turned out to be friendly, approaching us and offering us a goat to eat.

Later on in our journey I burnt my hand when boiling a billy for tea. In attempting to start a small fire after putting a few handfuls of sand into a tin and pouring some petrol onto the sand, something went wrong. A quick trip on the back of a military police motorbike to the nearby field hospital soon had the blisters popped and the damage repaired.

An occupational hazard for billy boilers - survived.

Meanwhile, the 7th Armoured Division supporting the advance was travelling the same road; however no offer of help was extended to our stranded truck crew. Since the promised truck did not appear, the three of us took off by foot until we reached an old vehicle dump controlled by the 7th Armoured.

For two days we pleaded with the guards at the vehicle yard, "Could you give us one of your wrecks so we can get to Tripoli, we have no other way to get there."

Eventually we were offered an old Dodge Utility vehicle.

The next stage of the journey recommenced after we returned to the broken down truck to retrieve intelligence papers. Travelling on to Derna, a short stop was made there. I had a chance to observe some of its ancient architecture - mainly underground water ways and reservoirs built by the Romans. Observing these sites provided a welcome interlude to chasing enemy soldiers.

The Germans were now in full retreat. Our Allied forces attempted to take the advantage and overpower the retreating troops. This would not be a simple and straight forward exercise and so it proved. Earlier, at Sidi Haneish, I remember a storm brewing up. Even in the deserts of the Middle East it can rain and cause conditions to deteriorate. Because the desert consists mainly of dust like sand and scattered rocks, rain can quickly turn the terrain into a bog. Our attacking Allied units became bogged down in mud, the elements conspiring to give the enemy a further chance to reorganise and so escape the immediate danger. The conditions experienced here bought time for the Axis forces to put miles between them and us - the chasing forces.

The desert chase. (Source: NZETC - Author: Loughnan, R. J. M.)

Climbing up Halfaya Pass. (Source: NZETC - Author: Walker, Ronald)

The winding road up Halfaya Pass. (Source: NZETC - Author: Walker, Ronald)

Apart from sporadic skirmishes chasing the German retreat back to Tripoli, the action at Halfaya was the last major action I would see in the war.

Tripoli

Days passed by as our troops marched onwards. At night we dug fox holes in the sand, sleeping in boots and covering ourselves in our great coats for protection against the night cold all the while watching out for scorpions. Lying in our fox holes we would gaze at the star lit desert skies allowing a little time for lonely wonder, as we had done on many nights before. Looking skywards I saw black silhouettes of German bombers crossing the moon and stars, the hum of their engines disturbing the beauty. It was the 'miss' in the drone of the engines that indicated to me that these were enemy planes.

We would park a dozen or so Bren Carriers in a circle, called a 'laga'. Our men slept inside this circle. To protect the men from marauding German soldiers, four guards rotated in four-hourly shifts.

The 'fox hole' – our bed in the cold desert night – boots stayed on. Rocks evident here and under them were...(Source: 'Sleeping in the desert', URL: http://www.nzhistory.net.nz/media/photo/sleeping-desert, (Ministry for Culture and Heritage), updated 6-Apr-2011)

Just on the outskirts of Tripoli near Homs, an army lorry tossed out a bag of flour and a box of sultanas along with some lard. Finding a courtyard, we captured a fry pan and a gas cooker. I proceeded to drum up some pan cakes much to the delight of comrades around me including a soldier from the Free French. It did not take long to exhaust the 50lb sack of flour. Plates were not needed.

I heard more, "I'll have some of those" requests than I had ever heard before.

As the cook I had gained instant popularity and not for the first time in my life! Not difficult to imagine after living for months on bully beef and 'dog biscuits.' The biscuits we were issued with were so hard that whenever we could we would soak them overnight in our Dixie cups before eating them.

Moving on a little further into Tripoli, our troops checking out streets and buildings for any signs of resistance came across vacated residences. We were aware of the contrasts seen all over the world between rich and poor and it was obvious here too. Finding one particular private residence, built more like a palace than a home, we decided to reside there and bathe in its luxury for a few days. Sleeping in sandy desert foxholes was soon to be forgotten. Casting our eyes on red satin covered Chesterfield suites, tiled marble floors and silver and gold taps, the next few days' accommodation was booked there and then. Our feet were put up for two nights sleeping on the suites and looking up at the crystal chandeliers. The only thing missing was the butler. Officers cut short this luxury ordering us out before the third night, worried that such richness would distract us from our purpose. War had not ended.

The episode we were experiencing was just a lull in hostilities. Italy lay in wait for most. Disappointed as we were about having to leave our new found luxury we had to go on to our next base - an army camp just outside Tripoli. The camp was to be made up of personnel from the many different units who had been involved in Egypt and in the push to Tripoli. I ended up in what I remember as a large old building, possibly an old school building.

We remained in Tripoli for some three months, being on call and in reserve. It was a time for more contemplation, sometimes bewilderment and thoughts about what we had experienced and what was still to come. With this lull in hostilities more entries were written in my Events Book. These expressed my comrades' personal feelings; one or two are noted below.

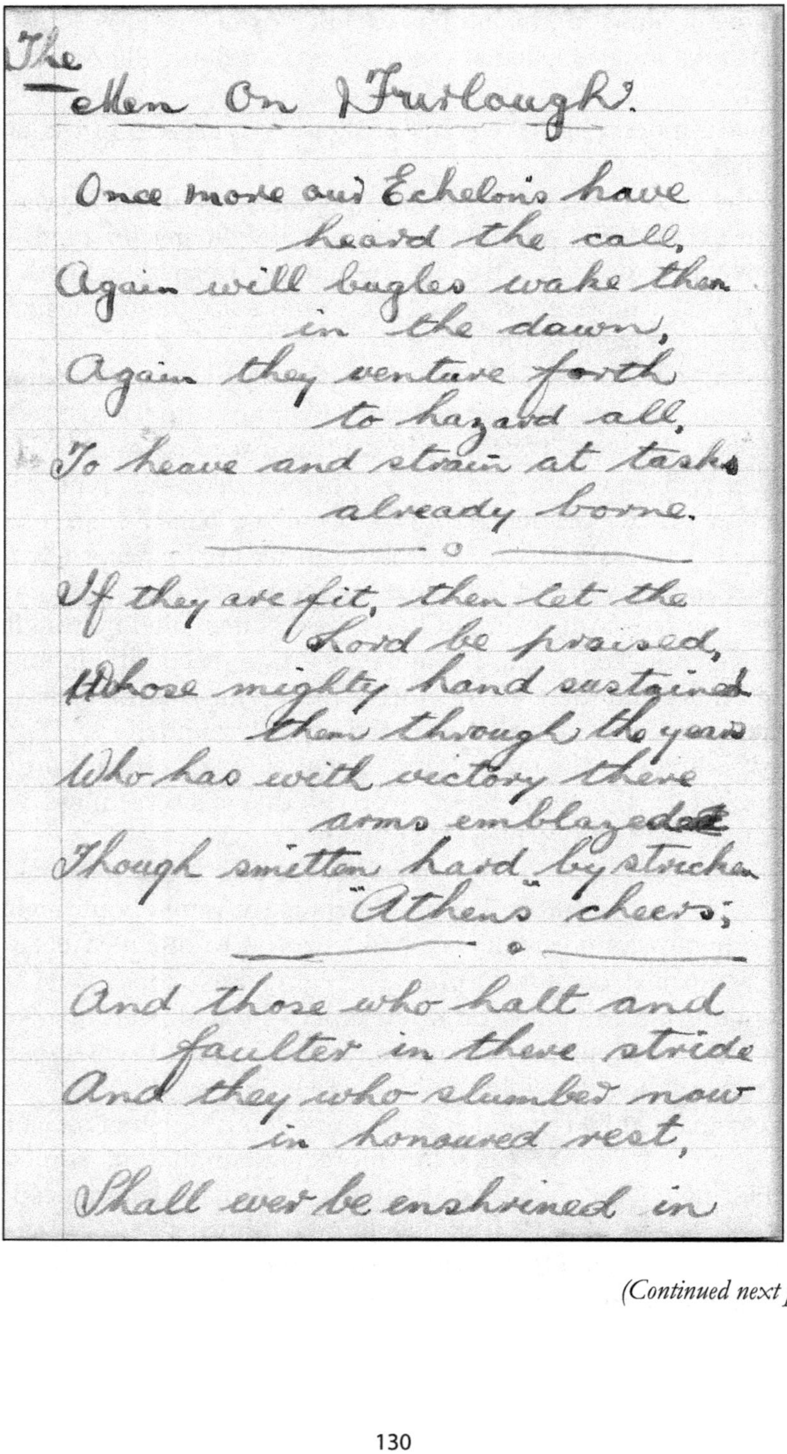

The Men On Furlough.

Once more our Echelons have
　　　heard the call,
Again will bugles wake them
　　　in the dawn,
Again they venture forth
　　　to hazard all,
To heave and strain at tasks
　　　already borne.

―――― o ――――

If they are fit, then let the
　　　Lord be praised,
Whose mighty hand sustained
　　　them through the years
Who has with victory their
　　　arms emblazed
Though smitten hard by stricken
　　　"Athens" cheers;

―――― o ――――

And those who halt and
　　　faulter in their stride
And they who slumber now
　　　in honoured rest,
Shall ever be enshrined in

(Continued next page)

> hallowed pride
> Within New Zealand's deep and
>   throbbing breast.
> ———
> And those who go again in to
>   the flame
> With bravest "Freyberg's" spirit
>   they will blend.
> To cleanse the weeping earth and
>   to proclaim.
> Goodwill and Peace to all
> (July - Jan) men, at the end
> 1943   R.S.M.   Huck

Men on Furlough

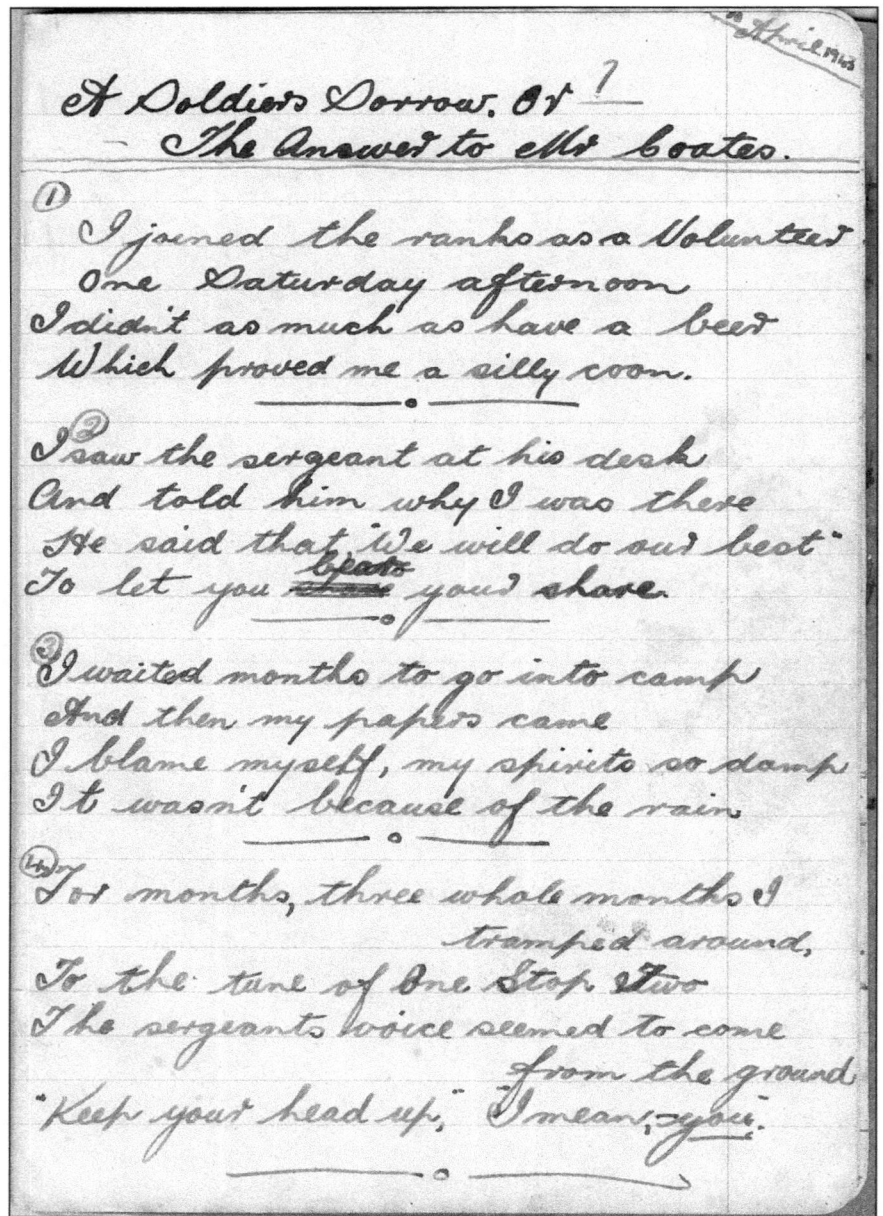

A Soldier's Sorrow

Along with any of my fellow soldiers who volunteered to come with me, I would journey to the outskirts of Tripoli at night to escape the incessant noise and rattling windows as Germans continued to bomb targets within the city – these were mainly isolated German raids. During one sporadic German night attack, a British ammunitions ship was bombed, causing a terrible bang which shook my socks off and rocked the whole of Tripoli. I went out to deserted mud huts made by Arab workmen, to escape the madness. The best way I can describe these huts would be 'shacks'. The feeling of being on my own comforted me, so I took advantage of the occasions when opportunities to be alone presented themselves.

Maybe in this we again see something of the 'loner' Pop had in him. Do we all have a little of the loner in us? I think the 'loner' part of Pop has mysterious elements we may wonder about and try to understand, and maybe we get to understand a little about this, but they remain with Pop – a part of the unknown.

A furlough (leave of absence) was to be granted to selected soldiers. Lucky to be one of the 10% chosen I finally had a definite direction set out for me. There was no loud or obvious rejoicing, however I very quickly began to ponder about what I would do back home now that being a soldier was to no longer play a part of my life. I had developed close friendships in harsh environments and on the battlefields of war and it didn't take long for me to realise that these friendships would be hard to hold onto, as most comrades would now be going their own way. Another factor which caused me unease and some distress concerned my feelings about home. Could I just slip back into a domestic home life, already strained by my previous relationships with my family? Reservations surfaced about leaving comrades behind, realising that for them the fighting would continue and many would not be returning home. I was headed home, away from war.

My Medals: NZ Defence Medal, The Africa Star (2nd left), War Medal (1939-45), 1939 – 1945 Star, NZ War Service Medal, and 8th Army Clasp (top)

FURTHER BACKGROUND

- Under 8th Army, General Bernard Montgomery takes Tripoli - 23rd January.
- March 20-28 – 8th Army breaks through the Mareth line
- March 27 – NZ Division executes 'left hook' at Tebaga Gap
- 13 May – German and Italian troops surrender in North Africa
- 15 May – NZ Division returns from Tunisia to Egypt
- 12 February 1944 – NZ Corps relieve 2nd US Army Corps at Casino

After three months in Tripoli, the long 3000 kilometre journey via army truck back to Maadi began. The dark black tar of the highway and the bright blue Mediterranean ocean once again painted colours in my eyes, as it did when I first saw it on arriving in Egypt. But there was no singing, the mood was solemn, too many dead bodies seen. More questions to ask, to add to those not yet answered. My contribution to the war effort was now at an end, I should have felt victorious or proud, yet I did not. And what was to happen now? It proved to be a long journey back.

Maadi had seen a lot of me and I had seen a lot of Maadi. Once back there, final preparations started for my journey home. Departing Maadi in truckloads, surrounded by hustle and bustle, a mix of emotions prevented clear thought. At Port Tewfik a converted passenger ship, the 'Nieuw Amsterdam', waited for its passengers. I was one of them. She may well have been a beautiful passenger ship in her previous life, however we were in no state at all to appreciate that beauty.

The Nieuw Amsterdam. (Source: permission from, "Provided by www.ssmaritime.com)

Although as soldiers we were relieved to be going home after our dramatic experiences in Greece and Egypt, the German propaganda machine was not about to let us go without firing a few parting shots. Lord Haw Haw surfaced again broadcasting on German radio warning us that our Japanese friends would be 'waiting for the Nieuw Amsterdam with submarines,' waiting to sink her on her return. Up to 3,000 returning troops were allocated to the Nieuw Amsterdam. The Dutch destroyer Van Trump, provided us with an escort on our journey home. After an unadventurous sail, things changed as we reached the Australian Bight (Perth through to the Bass Strait) where the ship experienced mountainous seas, as tall as houses.

Glad to reach Wellington, it was straight on to a train to Auckland where dad Charles and Annie were waiting to greet their returning soldier son. I had not expected family to be at the station. Not sure why really. My thoughts had been focused on the uncertainties of returning to civilian life and on returning to work, should I be lucky enough to find a job. Our family, reunited once more drove back in Charles' car.

Apart from a few, "No doubt, you are glad to be back" and "Now you can look forward to settling down", the trip back did not explode with chatter. Maybe that was to be expected.

Back home, Annie had prepared a full meal - one of a roast and cabbage. Dad Charles had welcomed me back but conversation did not flow freely between us.

I was away on active war duty from 1940 to 1943, in service of my country. Just as it was a momentous change for me going into a war I knew nothing about, another significant change was about to greet me as I tried to settle down on my return home.

CHAPTER 5

END OF WAR YEARS AND A RETURN TO SHADDOCK STREET

My return to civilian life was always going to throw up a few challenges for me. The years at war had given me experiences I never envisaged prior to sailing to Egypt from Wellington. Comradeships built up over the three years I was there had been abruptly broken; being together far away from home in foreign countries and in testing conditions was suddenly no longer.

Back home in New Zealand, I felt that the public didn't understand how to react with returning soldiers and that they acted selfishly, expecting us just to fit in with what they perceived to be the proper behaviour. There were ticker parades when we soldiers left, then on our return all we got were seven day acknowledgements in newspapers and the like. For me, I was living life in a daze, looking for mates in the street and in taverns because at least they would understand. At other times I sought out occasions to be alone. Trying to slip back into normal family life proved to be a difficult task, made more so due to reverberations I still felt from leaving home as a young lad.

Back in the family home, I was introduced to Edie (Billy's wife). I recall Edie and her mother-in-law chasing each other round the table. Part of the reason for doing this seemed to be their eagerness in trying to create a happy homecoming for me.

Shortly after, Annie began asking me strange questions, enquiring "Do you have eyes for Edie?"

"No way," I replied.

"But I can see it," she repeated.

"Go on," I resigned.

I had no intention of saying any more on this subject.

It wasn't an easy time at home. Apart from feeling like a lost son and missing my war mates there was what I perceived as Billy Beesley's favoured treatment within the family situation. My 'loner' desires were still niggling at me. Maybe being on my own was best for me. I thought about ways I could return to being a loner. Much talk and sympathy surrounded Billy when he returned home about a month after I returned from the Middle East. The focus on Billy's exploits, much of it which I felt was exaggerated, relegated my own experience to the background. Billy, a bit of a skite liked to tell stories of how with the NZ 3rd Division, he engaged the Japanese when in fact I believe little action would have taken place while he was stationed at Green Island. The urge to leave an uncomfortable Shaddock Street persisted.

> *When Japan entered the war in December 1941, the New Zealand Government raised another expeditionary force know as the 2nd N.Z.E.F. (I.P) for service in the Pacific, with the Allied Pacific Ocean Areas command. This force supplemented existing garrison troops in the South Pacific. The main fighting formation of the 2nd N.Z.E.F. (I.P.) comprised the New Zealand 3rd Division. However, although the 3rd Division never fought as a formation; its component brigades became involved in semi-independent actions as part of the Allied forces in the Solomon Islands, Treasury Islands and Green Island.*

(Source=http://en.wikipedia.org/wiki/military_history_of_NZ _during_World_War_11)

Missing army life, I would go out visiting local taverns trying to find old army mates to associate with. Life in Auckland felt foreign, more so than the foreign places I had just returned from. It was a different world and I found it difficult to adjust. It was in this context, after being back at home with Charles and Annie for some two months that I met up with an ex-army mate – Ken Rodgers, after Ken had called in at Shaddock Street. Ken had asked me to find an apartment with him.

It was at this time that an argument developed between my father Charles and me. I told Charles "You always treat Billy with more respect than you do with me, I feel like a second class citizen here at home."

I can't recall how father reacted to what I said. I felt he still harboured misgivings about my earlier running away from home. Thinking back, I don't think he ever really wanted me to leave home, not the first time nor on this occasion. However, for the second time I decided to leave Shaddock Street. I left with uncertainties, not knowing if I had made the right decision.

The next few months I spent flatting with Ken in a Lower Symonds street apartment complex. Ken was on the lookout for a Government subsidised farm block when, without warning, he suddenly left for Wellington. I lost all contact with Ken after he left. Once more I returned to Shaddock Street.

Letters continued to be received from the army requesting the return of my army uniform. Earlier I had received an army check for £129. There seemed some irony in the fact that we were offered money to buy clothes at the same time as being asked to return our army uniforms.

At this time, unbeknownst to me, my brother Jack had returned from London where he had been sent as a reinforcement to replace soldiers returning to New Zealand. Since the war had already finished, Jack did not see any action in England. Whereas I had volunteered, Jack was conscripted into the army. Jack had been living at home when called to London and he had returned to Shaddock Street on completion of his service. Jack was easy to get on with. Alma and Irene had left home at this stage. With the family increasing in number again as soldier sons returned from their overseas postings, sleeping options had to be reassessed. A bedette in the kitchen consisting of a pull down wire bed attached to the wall became my allocated sleeping quarters.

While my own bachelor status was about to change, it was in this period and soon after, that the Knill siblings would themselves be leaving the Knill home. At various stages over the next few years Alma, Irene, Jack and Ernie and then Billy and Owen married and moved away from home. I attended Ernie's church wedding but I do not recall being at any of my other siblings weddings. Alma likely married while I was overseas however I cannot recall when. Jack married in a registry office. Likewise, I can't remember Irene's, Billy's, and Owen's weddings.

Meanwhile, little did I know it but I was heading towards my own nuptials.

CHAPTER 6

COURTING – MARRIAGE – HOMES & FAMILIES

Although living in the Symonds Street apartments with Ken, I continued paying visits back home to Shaddock Street. It was after one such visit that Ken started talking about the Crystal Palace dance hall.

"How about we have a night out at the dances," Ken suggested.

Not super keen on chasing after the ladies I was non-committal. "Maybe some other time," I suggested.

"But we should go," Ken replied, not wanting to leave it at that, "if you won't come with me I'll go on my own."

"But I don't have any fancy clothes, Ken."

"That doesn't matter, we'll go in our army gear, the ladies are sure to be impressed with that."

"OK Ken, you win."

"Good on you Charlie."

Little did I know it, but things were about to change in bigger ways than I realised. Arriving at the Crystal Palace in resplendent army uniform (the ones that should have been returned!) along with sturdy army boots (*how good were they for dancing?*) the two of us stood at the door peering into the dance room. You can just imagine it! The music was playing, Pat McMinn was singing, the Epi Shalfoon Band playing, and two nervous soldiers stood, waiting at the entrance.

Something had to give otherwise we may have stood there all night.

I felt Ken's elbow dig into my ribs, "Over there, Charlie, see the two ladies dancing on their own?"

"Where?" I pretended.

"Let's go Charlie."

Plucking up the courage or whatever it took, we joined the two ladies and danced a dance together.

The army boots as heavy as they were tried to glide across the shiny kauri floor in sync with the music but the boots appeared to stick to the floor, not seeming to want to move. After one solitary dance we all headed over to the tables for a sit down. A couple of hours were spent chatting until closing time at midnight. The evening ended as we gentlemen went one way and the ladies went their way.

The Crystal Palace - 1953

The two ladies were Eileen and her sister Lorraine.

Back at home, in the quiet moments I had to myself, I found myself starting to ponder on romantic liaisons with Eileen. I felt my heart flutter in a way it had not done before.

Sitting at the table an evening or two later, together with Jack, Ernie and Joyce (Ernie's wife) our chat turned to dancing at the Palace.

"Go and give Eileen a ring," urged Joyce.

I waited a day or two and then called Eileen. It was in the back of my mind that she might chase me away but she didn't and so we went off on our first 'real' date. I felt my proclamations that 'I wasn't into women' starting to change tack. More dates soon followed. Movies at the Tivoli picture theatre, Karangahape Road, near the Grafton Bridge end became the vogue. Trams were caught from Mt Eden into town, a 25 minute ride. At the back of the theatre, projector boxes beamed the movies onto the screen. The halftime intermission was the time to go and get an ice-cream and maybe a Jaffa ball. In these days ice creams were also sold at the aisles. Desperate men would buy a four penny ice-cream for their lady friends and zip outside for a quick cigarette before the half time interval finished, sometimes tripping over in the aisles in the dark on their way back if they took too long.

Having been introduced to cigarettes in Egypt and probably addicted by now, I had to tell Eileen, " Just a minute dear, I'll have a quick smoke and come back with your ice-cream."

After a short two months of romance I was already thinking of asking Eileen the question. Not bad I suppose for a man who only two months earlier had told Jack he was not too much into women! And romantic attachments didn't just happen, competition existed in the form of American soldiers who wooed our New Zealand women with flowers and a whole lot of accented sweet talk, all done accompanied with styled haircuts and finely pressed army uniforms. This behaviour apparently impressed our ladies, in contrast to the typical New Zealand man's approach of going on a date bringing along a bottle of beer. I was aware of such competition and had planned ahead, already having selected and purchased an engagement ring from Innes Jewellers on Queen Street. This cost me the princely sum of £75.

The next thing to do was pick the moment to ask the question. It was election day, the 25th September, 1943. There we stood at the romantic location of the Evan's front gate. It was around 5 o'clock in the afternoon and let's say that the sun was shining when, feeling good and confident, I plucked up the courage, took a deep breath and then let the words roll out, "Eileen, I want to ask you if we could become engaged?"

I did not hear a reply.

Eileen took off like a flightless bird around to the back of the house to find her mother and tell her the news. Meanwhile, I was left standing at the front gate wondering if I had said the right thing. I did not have to wait for long as from the kitchen window I heard Nan Evans call out, "Come on in Charlie."

Feeling a little apprehension I opened the front gate and walked down the path to the kitchen door.

As soon as I entered the house I was made welcome and the nervousness I had felt disappeared. Eileen's parents accepted me there and then as a new member in the Con and Ettie Evans (Nan) household.

There did not seem any need for an extended time for Eileen and I to get to know each other, or for trials or investigations. A long engagement appeared to serve no logical purpose. Not wasting any time therefore, our thoughts were directed towards a wedding. The year was 1943.

Moving ahead quickly, we got organised and laid out wedding plans. Con got onto planning all the logistical stuff. Eileen chose the venue - St David's of Khyber Pass, Church of England, as the church for our nuptials. Nan Evans did what she did best and started with an ambitious baking plan.

My best man was to be Pat Hickey, my railway colleague from Maungaturoto. With all the arranging and organising to be done, there was no time to stop and think and the big day quickly arrived.

During my life I had faced the odd confrontational situation. I never ran away from them. One of these happened at my wedding. Having had myself a beer or two, a photographer lent me a push, trying to make me look a bit tipsy so I reckoned. To me this nudge seemed to be a deliberate act. Since I was not sure if the man harboured any further aggressive tendencies, and rather than wait for further developments, I threatened to punch him one. Earlier in the day, Pat had started off celebrations with a few beers before the church service. Maybe a few were shared for old time's sake too. The drama didn't end there with the camera man either for I managed to drop the ring in the church. For a moment I thought I was in the movies. Eileen was not too impressed with these events and has remarked a few times since then, "you even had too many at our wedding".

The reception was held in St David's church hall. Nothing too fancy and after the telegrams were read, cakes, sandwiches and scones were enjoyed by all. Unfortunately someone had to pay the bill and that happened to be Con. Right from the start Eileen and I were not ones to venture too far afield - our honeymoon was celebrated over three or four days at a St Heliers Bay motel.

Married life had begun. At first Eileen and I lived at Con and Ettie's home at Wairiki Road, Mt Eden, for some 12 months. It was a busy place with Edwin, Lorraine, Daphne, Ron and a boarder all in the same house. Con and Ettie made us feel comfortable living there, and for me it felt better than living in the rather strained environment at Shaddock Street.

The boarder turned out to be an interesting character named Norman Jury, a 70 year old pensioner. Norm liked to talk a lot about WW2 (and other things!) commenting to me more than once,

"You guys were on a 'Cook's Tour' to England."

"Why do you say that, Norm?" I would ask.

"It was just a trip away for you."

This situation didn't exactly encourage friendly relations and I think Norm's indifference may have stemmed from his lack of knowledge of war's reality or even from a certain degree of jealousy. Norm didn't seem to appreciate my presence at home and he always seemed to be 'gibing' me whenever he had the chance. Making wisecracks about the war, as if he knew everything, tested my metal no end.

The relationship between the Evan's children and us as newlyweds worked well. We all sat round the dinner table in the evenings enjoying Nan's cooking, including Norman who couldn't wait to pull out the poker cards.

"Poker time," he would beckon.

It seems that for Norm, poker was a way of supporting his income. Did he always win? I'm not sure if he did.

Big meals of cabbage and potatoes were served, sometimes with lamb. Sunday was cake day.

Ernie had married Joyce Woolley while I was overseas. Joyce came from Con's side of the family, thus was a cousin to Eileen.

Joyce and Ernie visited on Sundays, tagging along with them were Joyce's mum and dad. There was a feeling that it was Nan's delightful cakes and scones that brought them back there for their regular Sunday visits. At the time I thought that visiting relations just to eat was not a very neighbourly thing to do. Time has taught me to see it a little differently in that even if it was true, would it really have mattered anyway? Whatever, they certainly enjoyed a fair swag of the cakes on offer and Nan had the chance to serve a bunch of happy customers.

Eileen and I with Len – about one year old, at Wairiki Road, 1948-note the Tecoma hedge in the background- wetas lived in this hedge.

The Evans Family

Con and Ettie Evans lived at Wairiki Road until Nan moved to a unit in Mt Roskill a few years after Con died. The rented Wairiki house was an 80 year old, high ceiling weatherboard home. In its earlier history the home had once caught on fire, after which the scarred and charred weatherboards were simply turned inside out and renailed. Rats, plenty of them, had also made this their home. Baths were taken in hot water heated from a gas fired califont – a cylinder fixed to the wall above the bath. Before you got any water you had to place a shilling in the meter. The copper stove was used to boil up the water needed for washing clothes. The washing was done in an outside shed.

With Len a little while later. Still wearing my prized church coat – how did it survive the intervening years?

This rather large house had five bedrooms. There was a sitting room with a piano in it, the piano played mostly by Nan. A solid looking Shacklock iron stove was stacked with coke or coal in preparation for cooking the evening meal. Nan's more than capable baking skills certainly helped keep the family alive.

Con was known for his love of cigarettes and horse racing. Placing bets with the bookies was one reason the telephone received so much use, particularly on Saturdays.

One of my jobs at Wairiki Road was to trim the Tecoma hedges (the hedge with the wetas in them) and another was to dig up the vegetable garden. On the entertainment side, Eileen and I would sometimes attend the races at Ellerslie. Many a gambling habit had its early origins at Wairiki Road.

Portrait of Evans and Woolley families.
Front row; Myrtle Woolley (nee Evans)on knee, Joyce Woolley (now Knill), Ivy Powley (nee Evans) with children Percy and Leonard, and Gladys Ettie Evans (nee McKenzie) with daughter Eileen Gladys Evans.

Len was born at Wairiki Road. Ettie doted on Len, her arms always ready to hold her first grandchild. Con passed away of cancer on New Zealand Cup day 1948. Even then he was heard asking,

"Who won the cup?"

When told it was Sir Garnish he nodded as if to say,

"Told you so."

Nan Evans (Gladys Ettie Evans, nee McKenzie, whose mother Sarah Ann Collett was part of the Collett racing family) is remembered as a caring old soul who loved having visitors and family call in on them.

I (Lou) remember visiting her with Sandra at her unit just off the Mt Roskill end of Dominion Road. The sun shone in through the front window, the racing guide, Best Bets lay on the coffee table, the scones decorated with jam and cream and the casual conversation relaxed and amicable. Then a little dinner, put on the table, not flash but yum anyway. Nan gave everybody fond and simple memories to hold on to and treasure. I have these.

Nan passed away at Greenlane Hospital of a heart attack at around 70 years of age. She had gone off on a walk to do a little shopping and had forgotten to take her heart pills with her.

Con and Ettie brought up a family of five, three daughters and two sons. Of these Eileen was the oldest, born in 1922. Then came Edwin, born 1924; Lorraine, born 1926; Daphne, born 1931; and finally Ronald (Ronnie), who was born in 1935.

Nan – Ettie Evans with Lorraine and Ray Scorror.

Daphne met and married Ron Peckham and they had two children, Laurie and Evelyn. Lorraine married Ray Scorror and they had three children, Julie, Robert and Irene. Ronald (Ron or Ronnie) married Antoinette Wattam-Bell (Toni) and they had four children: Colin, Blair, Vivian and Cydne. Ron's interest was greyhound racing. He was appointed president of the Auckland Greyhound Club in 1970. Toni maintained an interest in horse racing and later in researching family history. Cydne became a horse trainer and trained a Wellington Cup winner Cyclades (2002). (Thoroughbred News, 20 June 2003)

Daphne and Ron Peckham lived in Te Atatu while Lorraine and Ray Scorror lived in Wanganui. Ron and Toni Evans lived on a small farm in Dairy Flat. Auckland. The Evans clan celebrated family Sundays with many an outing to Auckland's Long Bay. Here the yarns flowed freely, the children played and swum in the ocean and Nan's baking laid out and tasted. Custard pies for my delight. I loved those things! Nan made these from real eggs and custard.

I have fond personal recollections of family life amongst the Evans clan. Lorraine had an easy going nature, conversation came naturally to her. Daphne was also a lovely lady, easy to talk to and Sandra and I were privileged to have been able to visit her on the spur of the moment just a week or two before Daphne passed away in April, 1994. It was via Ron that a love of greyhound and horse racing developed for many of the Evans' clan and for me. I particularly remember two greyhounds Ron raced. Minstrel Boy raced in the Auckland Cup and Supermatic raced as a hurdler. It was at the Kumeu greyhound track where illegal betting became a criminal behaviour I engaged in. The memories of going down to the car park at the back of the track, car windows being wound down (quickly), money transferring hands and then a quick wind up of the window just before the next race started still tickles the excitement buzz. Nan Evans never forbade such a thing; as a matter of fact she often operated the window winders! This was how the family organised its betting; once the money was collected, a delegated member of the family ran over to the 'course bookmaker' to have the bets placed. Toni and daughter Cydne have continued the racing vein, still training horses today. Today in Rotorua, our son David, races greyhounds in partnership with Scotty Payne in Rotorua. I continue to have the occasional flutter.

Evans family – Robbie, Julie, Ray, Eileen, Len, Keith, Pop, Lorraine & Irene – holidays in Gisborne, about 1955.

A rather sad fact was that Daphne, Lorraine and Ronnie all passed away before reaching 60 years of age. That Eileen reached 89 years is a benchmark achievement all of its own.

Tutuki Street, Waterview, and Avondale

With Len having been born while we were at Wairiki Road and with our family growing, it was time to start looking for a home of our own. Con encouraged us to apply to State Advances for a state rental property. I applied, however the wheels of bureaucracy turned slowly and so we waited, and waited, for a response. Con pushed me to keep pestering SAC. Looking for ways to speed up the process it was to be Eileen's brother Ted's situation which would lead us to finding a successful outcome. Ted, serving in the New Zealand Air Force, had applied for overseas war service, desperately wishing to fly aircraft in England and Europe. However his application was rejected due to Ted's tuberculosis. I asked Ted if we could raise the issue of his tuberculosis with State Advances. What we wanted to do was notify State Advances that we had a baby (Len) living in the same house as Ted and that we were worried about the risk that tuberculosis posed. The strategy worked and we were soon allocated a property in Tutuki Street, Avondale. We lived here for three years. The two bedroom house became too small when Keith was expected. Another application was made to State Advances, this time for a three bedroom house. After a further wait an offer came in for a property in Mt Roskill.

7 Milliken Road, Mt Roskill

It was not long before we got a letter notifying us that a state house at 7 Milliken Road was available. This house was to be our second home. And it was – for 25 years! It was later sold for $26,000.

Initially we rented the state house for four or five years. When Government policy changed, allowing tenants to apply to purchase their rented properties, we decided this would be a good opportunity to buy our first home. It certainly turned out to be a beneficial move for us. Given a State Advances Loan of £1800 at 3% interest the house was paid off before we moved on to a unit in Sandringham. We certainly enjoyed our years at 7 Milliken Road.

Our street would have been typical of New Zealand residential living; families with children, wife at home, husbands out to work, children playing together, gardens and vegetables, cars in driveways (not all mobile), a few neighbourhood disputes, noise here and there, fish 'n chips, barbecues, newspaper delivery, bills in the letterbox, lawn mowing and mortgages.

One major project I took on was an upgrade of the concrete tile roof. Ignoring hazards associated with working at height I wire brushed every single concrete tile and there were many! My knuckles were bared and fingers suffered from cramp. More than one wire brush wasted away. Then each tile was lovingly painted green. Completed, it was a job to be proud of, the number one house on the street.

It is possible that the shining new roof led to a bit of jealousy being felt by the Martins next door. A feud already existed between Mrs Martin and Eileen. The Martins had two children, a son and a daughter who sometimes played with Len and Keith. No animosity existed at all between the children but with adults it is sometimes a different story.

Mrs Martin was a Samoan lady. Mr Martin a European. Life did not always run smoothly for the Martins, not helped by the father's preferences for alcoholic beverages. It was not unusual for Mrs Martin to stand on her property, hands on hips and stare directly at Eileen. At some point in proceedings, along the shortcut pathway to Mt Albert Road, Eileen was pushed. If Mrs Martin talked to neighbours up the road, Eileen would harbour suspicions that they would be talking about her. Not the best of situations, neighbours on the lookout for each other and always on their toes.

The home at 7 Milliken Road, Mount Roskill- and the garage.

The weekly grocery shop usually involved a visit to the local Four Square. Choices in the mid-1900s were limited. No big brand food stores yet. The Four Square chain would be the forerunner to the large supermarket stores which saw off the traditional family grocer and home deliveries. The IGA grocery chain was also around at that time. And gone would be the telephoned grocery order. Personal service disappeared in favour of the checkout counter. Our shopping was done nearby in Mt Roskill. Every week Eileen would walk along to the Four Square and purchase our usual goodies; bread, milk, Weetbix, peanut butter, sardines and our favourite herrings in tomato sauce The grand total of our grocery bill in the 1950s was around two to three pounds.

The Four Square Grocery shop – one in nearly every town. The one on the left at Kingsview a short walk from Wairiki St – 1940s. (Source: Auckland War Memorial Museum Library - Outside D. Smith's Four Square store in Kingsview Road, Mt Eden. 1940s? - window display, old pram, woman waiting in hat and gloves on the footpath background left.)

Eileen liked to look good. Looking good didn't worry me that much. To stay with the fashion she would tag me along to Farmers in Hobson Street in the central city. We would park the children in the children's playground on the top floor while Eileen shot into the men's and women's clothing department. I followed, however after five minutes of ruffling through women's clothing my impatience unsettled Eileen and she excused me to the hardware department. I do remember dungarees (blue denims) going for around five shillings.

My building talents were shown off when I decided to modify our lean-to carport into a 'modern' garage. My new design, constructed with wooden frame, a flat roof and fibrolite sides looked pretty flash. The garage initially had a canvas tie down sheet as its front door - this I later replaced with a two way folding door, painted green.

The 14 year old Bon Chretien pear tree story is worth telling. This tree received my loving care for many years yet it never returned a reward for all this care and attention. It refused to blossom! Neither gardening publications nor neighbourhood gardening networks offered any solutions to my problem. Then one day (after 14 years), on the wharf, a mate told me that I needed to cut the tap root. Presto! Next year blossoms decorated the tree in white.

Our Children

Len was born at Bethany's on Mt Eden Road while Eileen and I were still living at Wairiki Road. Keith and Sandra were born while at Milliken Road. All our children received schooling at Roskill Primary School on Dominion Road, Mt Roskill Intermediate on Pah Road and then Mt Roskill Grammar High School on Bremmer Road.

Len, with a special character all of his own (as all babies have), provided his parents with a fair amount of run around. A sociable young lad he had no trouble mixing with the local neighbourhood boys even if some happened to show a few mischievous tendencies from time to time. Gifted with a musical talent, guitars were strummed at home and belted out with more ferocity along with the drums in the Haresnapes garage. A visit from the men in blue to the Milliken home one morning related to an incident the police were checking out. Apparently, the previous evening, three or four young lads had been seen conducting a few experiments with sheep up on a high point along the bays. With the constable about to speak, Eileen sent Sandra off to be invisible but she resisted, wanting to see how the policeman went about the interviewing process.

"Mrs Knill, we believe your son may have been involved in an incident last night where some sheep were tipped over a bluff."

Eileen was stunned and she didn't, or couldn't, say anything.

"Could that have involved your son, Mrs Knill?"

"I don't think so, officer," said a blushing Eileen, realising she had to say something. Now indignant and with her face turning red she wished this wasn't happening.

Len knew what the story was and took off for his emergency shelter under the house, not intending to emerge for quite some time.

After a two way exchange between Eileen and the constable it seems that culpability could not be established and the matter ended there.

"Just as well," Eileen seemed to mutter to herself.

The shock tactic employed by the police seemed to work on Len, the fear of jail too much for him.

Len was not aware that the police officer had taken me aside and said "Don't be too hard on the lad."

I reckoned that Len may have been in for a lot more trouble than a simple telling off had the constable been mean.

Len worked at Steel Brothers, a local sheet metal business. He met and married Beverly Cryer. They had two children, Cherrie and Robbie. They moved to the Gold Coast of Australia in 1980 after Len was made redundant and at around the same time having had their home burgled. Australia has been their home since moving there.

Keith was the second born. He refused to give his parents any trouble.

His main claim to fame as a young fella had to do with sticking a steel knitting needle into an element in the oven causing an explosion. Shocked, he proceeded to scream his heart out. A lucky lad he was, not to have been injured or electrocuted. The State Advances repair man soon determined that the damage had not occurred via a 'natural event' Even a four year old learns lessons and Keith never tried to repeat the exercise. He has never taken up knitting!

The three 'angelic' Knill children – about 1956 - Len, Sandra, and Keith

After leaving school Keith gained a position at The Auckland Star as an apprentice printer. His mum, Eileen, took him to the Star office after seeing an ad asking for; 'a youth wanted with a view to apprenticeship.' Actually Keith had little choice in the matter, his mother determined that he never be jobless. Many editions of the then evening newspaper and later the morning *Herald* passed by his watchful eye. Keith provided a dutiful service to Auckland and New Zealand newspaper readers over a lifetime of work. Keith met Christine Logan and they have two children, Steven, an electrician currently living in Perth, Australia, and Katrina, working with the NZ Department of Conservation and currently living in Tauranga. Christine has worked in the banking business for many years, in later years working in Wellsford.

Sandra, like her brother Keith, refused to give her parents any major trouble. On leaving Mount Roskill Grammar she worked at Motor Traders in Cook Street and at Freightways in Mt Eden and later at Wormald's in New Lynn. Sandra met Lou at the Monaco Dance Hall in Auckland. Her only claim to fame was staying out late with Lou which annoyed the traditionally held beliefs of Eileen. Her mini skirts caused her mum and dad to seriously question the current fashion. It mattered little that they suited her. Sandra and Lou's children were; Claudine, David, Kim, Michael and Karen. Claudine became a fulltime house manager, David a certified machinist at Carter Holt Harvey, Kim has been working in the Emergency Department at Rotorua Hospital, Michael at Richmond

Foods and studying IT at Waiariki Polytechnic and Karen working at Bunnings prior to starting a Veterinarian Nurses programme.

Eileen and I are proud of our children, their various achievements and proud also of the families they have raised and the grandchildren, precious gifts indeed.

Having gone to war and having returned back home, then having met up with and marrying Eileen, and with our young family growing bigger, whatever 'loner' instinct still resided in me, it was time to turn my attention to developing plans for settling down. To achieve this, my first efforts had to be geared to finding a long term job that would help to support my family. I knew that this would be a very big change for me.

Many a family loses touch with each other, some completely, as life moves along its course. Fortunately our respective families have always found means and methods of keeping in touch, not as much as there should have been maybe but enough to maintain contact and be interested in how each is living. Pop felt a yearning to capture his memories and tell his story (this story).

CHAPTER 7

WORKING LIFE AFTER THE WAR

Now that I was back home after the war had ended for me, finding a job that fitted in with a new life was a high priority and I had to attend to it. Having worked on North Island farms and for the New Zealand Railways at Mercer and Maungaturoto, I felt that these jobs did not offer the permanency I was looking for even though it was work I mostly enjoyed. The difference between being a farm hand and owning your own farm was a bridge too far for me. Owning a farm really didn't enter my thought patterns.

Possessing a determination instilled in me from my life experiences and from a tough upbringing, looking for work came naturally to me. Being overly fussy about which occupation I would choose was never really considered. Leaving school at 14, living through the depression years, experiencing war and difficult family circumstances meant that any job would be considered unless, of course, there were unusual circumstances such as at Hikutaia when the farmer offered me a job, but couldn't even start me off with a cup of tea.

Searching around for whatever work was available, I noticed the Auckland Wharfs advertising for men to do sea gulling work. I immediately applied for the position. It helped that preference was given to returned servicemen. The offer of sea gulling work did not mean permanent work, something I was looking for. To get this part time work, men were required to report to the wharf office each day to see if jobs were available. With a high likelihood of jobs being allocated to ex-army personnel, I was willing to catch the bus into town every day and register at the office. Wharf work would suit me I felt. Being amongst fellow workers, being able to lose myself in the crowd and with superior pay and bonuses to those I had received on the farm or at the Railways, I could see myself settling into this work. Still I was looking for a more permanent position so when a job came up working for Affco just across the road I took that. Meanwhile, I had applied with the wharf for a permanent position just to keep all bases covered.

Affco was located in a rather large concrete building across from King's wharf. Actually the daily grind was not too much different from that I had experienced at the wharf. No absence of manual labour either as 56 pound butter boxes had to be taken from refrigerators and stacked on rollers to be moved into railway wagons for the short journey to the waiting ships and transport on to Mother England. I stayed at Affco for some six months before deciding to move on once more.

The then Labour Government recognised that there would be difficulties providing work opportunities for the thousands of servicemen returning from the war. The government set up trade training centres, one of these in Tamaki. A few trades were represented including; painting, window glazing and carpentry work. To get returning servicemen into productive work as soon as possible the usual three to five year trade apprenticeship was condensed into a 12 month training course. The first two months were spent in the classroom, followed by supervised training in the field. Instructed in class by Harry, a gentleman with a felt hat and a beard, I furthered my education as with his kind permission he allowed me to practice mixing paints in his garage.

Having chosen the painting option and completing my classroom training I was ready to venture onto the practical aspects of the trade and to go out painting. A fellow trainee was fortunate enough to be asked to paint the inside of a church friend's house in Gladstone Road, Mt Albert, and he asked me to join him as second in charge. My 'boss' then went out and purchased a biscuit coloured paint which the owner had indicated he wanted. We painted a test piece on an old board and showed this to the owner.

"That's fine, exactly what I want," he said.

Having been given the go ahead after the owner informed us that he would be away for a couple of weeks we got stuck into painting.

This was a straight forward job requiring the interior walls to be painted. Pleased with the outcome of our first painting job we awaited the owners return. He did not see the finished job with the same pleasure as we did, "Sorry gentlemen," he said, "this is not the colour we agreed on, I am most disappointed."

"But it is a biscuit colour," we implored

As if to cut things off there and then, his sharp response was,

"Afraid not and please don't expect to be paid for this work."

After being out of pocket on our very first job we couldn't have made a worse start to our budding careers.

This ended my association with this trainee. Not for any particular reason other than I felt this might well happen again. I quickly pushed on to find something else. Responding to a tradesman's ad in the paper for a trainee painter, I found work painting a house in St Johns near Remuera. It's good to learn something new every day and here I discovered that cheap leadless paint could easily be purchased in a range of stores offering bargain basement priced paints. Being one never to invest my time and effort working on cheap jobs, I painted the outside of the house and then left it at that. Besides, the trade school had taught me how to become a quality tradesman and not a cheap service provider. The boss was no more, gone, the second one I had parted ways from.

Achieving job satisfaction in the painting trade was proving difficult. Maybe Frank Simpson was the man to offer me this opportunity. Frank visited Nan Evans at Wairiki Road. Being himself a painter, he had heard of the training which I had undergone and that I had already 'tried' a few painting jobs. He kindly took me on. Frank, incidentally, was a man of certain mysterious proportions since it was he, who rumour had it, may have had some sort of earlier association with Ettie. Whatever, it seems to have been an unknown which remained under wraps and was not openly discussed.

Painting went better with Frank. Together we completed quite a few jobs. Frank's experience seemed to earn him a band of happy customers. Frank chose his paint more carefully, using paint of a quality suited to the job. Still there were the odd misdemeanours, the odd use of leadless paint. A factor which kept painters in check in the early 1950s were the random site inspections from State Advances inspectors who were responsible for taking paint samples to check paint composition. Should too much turpentine be found in the sample repercussions would follow!

A common job done in those years involved making minor roof repairs using canvas stretched over the roof patch to be mended and covering it with black bitumen. On one particular job, after fixing a canvas piece over the hole, Frank fell through the patch, saving himself from a more serious fall by grabbing hold of the chimney stack. Being all of 18 stone, Frank would have hit the ground with a thud. From this point on I would be ordered onto the roof for any roof work. With Frank not being a designated trainer and with some dubious practices existing in the trade, I became discouraged with painting work. Even simple things such as boiling up the billy for our morning and afternoon cuppa could be an annoying pain in the backside since on some jobs home owners didn't have time to help us with that even. Not that every job was done on the cheap. Frank actually knew his trade well. After a couple of years of toiling with Frank and the painting business my meandering nature kicked in once more. I lost track of what happened to Frank but I do know that he moved to Australia once he finished painting.

The other issue with painting for me was the low wages. My income of around £10/week did not match what I could potentially earn on the wharfs. Having worked there earlier I had an appreciation of the pay rates being offered and so sought another opportunity there.

In 1954, such a possibility presented itself when a neighbour of mine in Milliken Road, Bruce Ellis, recommended me to the Auckland wharf employment office. I was duly employed and so began a 23 year working life on the Auckland wharfs, from 1954 until my retirement in 1977.

The major wharf strike of 1951 was still fresh in the memory of many people's minds, reverberations from the strike not auguring well for a comfortable working life, at least not to start off with. Irrespective of all that, I had decided on my next step. This one was to last for a long time.

Lou Geraets

Working Life on the Wharf, 1954 - 1977

The permanency I looked for in a job that also paid well was here, at the wharfs. Throughout my entire working life I spent much of it in jobs demanding a fair degree of manual labour. I was aware that this job would demand physical effort as well. With some certainty I can say that I never let any of my employers down. Another proud claim to fame was that I was never without a job.

The first few years on the wharf were spent unloading cargo ships berthed at any of the different wharfs stretched along Auckland's waterfront. A job no one asked for was working on the freezer boats. The tasks I had to look forward to on these boats involved lifting and stacking butter boxes, blocks of cheese and frozen lamb carcasses down in the holds. The freezing conditions were hated by all wharfies. Nobody looked forward to being allocated work on the freezer boats. To alleviate some of the cold, old sugar sacks were cut into strips, the strips formed around the feet and tied with rope up to and around the calf. Gloves, heavy jackets and woolly hats were essential wear. Innovation was the order of the day, a degree of resilience a necessity.

Then there were the wool ships – opposite conditions to the cold of the freezer ships. Hated almost as much as the cold, the hot and sweaty conditions deep in the holds of the wool ships tested our resolve. Workers allocated these boats soon had frowns on their faces. Double dumps – two 460 pound wool bales strapped together by double slings like lassoes, would be swung into position down into the hold. Terrible conditions in the summer heat of February months. Working here reminded me of the conditions I experienced marching through the heat of the desert sands in the war years. Sweat and smell became an occupational hazard. Working down in the holds was a good way to keep slim or lose weight - a bygone era now, as today all wool is baled into containers.

Fortunately, a variety of goods were exported from the wharfs. Had there been just the frozen meat and wool ships a man's working life at the Auckland wharfs would have been of short duration indeed.

Not that every other job was easy. Unloading soda ash, imported from Indonesia and used for making chinaware at Crown Lynn and sulphur, imported from Galveston USA, were also jobs I frowned upon ending up with. Issued with respirators, we had to shovel sulphur and soda ash away from the sides of the hold since it did not flow back freely into the middle pile where the 'grab' would come in and pick up its load.

Preferred jobs were wheat ships from Australia. Wearing simple gauze masks rather than the compulsory respirators worn on sulphur ships, less shovelling was needed as wheat flowed freely to the centre of the ship's hold. The grabber would load wheat into hoppers located near the ships. Trucks would collect the wheat from under the hopper.

Tea chests from India, Dinky Toys and razors imported from Germany were just some of the imported cargoes which were targeted by some wharfies who considered the contents of a few damaged boxes to be fair game or a 'perk' they were entitled to. It would surprise many to know how 'innovative' certain wharfies were in finding ways to become the new owners of illegally gained goods.

Loading waiting trucks with sand – Auckland Wharfs – 1948. I happened to do lots of preparation for this down in the holds. (Source: Unknown)

Asbestos wool boats arrived from Europe every six months or so. Bales, the size of conventional farm hay bales were unloaded from the ship's hold. Masks were used, however safety controls for handling asbestos were far laxer than they are today. In New Zealand, asbestos was used in the manufacture of fibrolite sheeting.

Sugar bags filled with potatoes came from the South Island by coastal traders. The Tofua carried bananas from the Islands and carrots arrived from Ohakune, collected at the wharf by Turners and Growers trucks. Car boats came in mainly from England and later from Japan, about once per month to Fergusson Wharf. These were the high bonus boats all wharfies wanted to be allocated to, the other bonus boats being the wheat and steel boats. Only once in all my years on the wharf was I allocated to a car boat, but the memory of driving Jaguar X2s and Bentleys from the boat to the wharf depot remains a pleasant one. Would I have loved to have been on more car boats and have driven more of these classy cars down the ramps!

Loading and unloading mail on Princess Wharf happened regularly. Three or four men would load and unload mail using large rope slings. Not a preferred job for me due to the sometimes heavy and awkward handling that had to be done with these canvas mail bags. Mail came in on passenger ships such as the Oriana or Mariposa.

Much of the work done on the wharfs was of a hazardous nature. Work on the steel boats, although these were the bonus-payment boats, brought with it additional dangers. Long steel rods or solid steel girders loaded in swinging slings presented many a serious risk of injury. Strains and sprains from manual handling and respiratory hazards from asbestos, ash and sulphur were ever-present hazards. We often took these risks for granted.

Then there were the different attitudes of supervisors. One particular supervisor, a Dutchman, was remembered for his keenness to get the job done, often overlooking safety concerns. His was a loud voice I remember well. Harbour Masters, not the most popular gentlemen on the waterfront were not exposed to the same level of hazards, they basically opened and shut doors and resided in offices. Many of these guys seemed to believe their position elevated them way above that of the mere 'wharfie'. One of these gentlemen issued warnings to my humble self on a number of occasions cautioning me,

"You don't know it yet but the day is coming when you won't be here, you will be made redundant."

"How do you know that?" I asked him with some scepticism.

"Wait and see," he replied, seeming to gain some confidence in telling me about his prediction.

I can tell you that this gentleman had it exactly right. He foresaw the impending containerisation boom which eventually resulted in dramatic job losses on the Auckland wharfs. Fortunately for me that time had not yet arrived and I had retired before these changes occurred.

Time keepers randomly appeared from out of the shadows during loading/unloading, catching any workers who may have downed tools early. Those caught out were sent home, suspended for two days without pay.

Auckland Waterfront – Princess Wharf, 1920s (mainly a passenger boat terminal, also mail drops). (Source: Sir George Grey Special Collections, Auckland Libraries 895-A59335)

Auckland Waterfront – showing the Ferry Buildings. (Source: Sir George Grey Special Collections, Auckland Libraries 1-W348)

Many wharfies shared common interests. Many had returned from fighting in the war, they enjoyed a beer or two, struggled with mortgages and looked forward to their annual holidays.

Sitting down having lunch one day, Harry, a Maori chap, offered me his bach at Maunganui in Northland.

"Charlie, I have a little bach up north, why don't you and your dear wife take a holiday up there?"

"That's nice of you Harry," I replied.

"Don't worry about the one or two rats that share the place," Harry added.

"Think I'll need to talk to Eileen about that."

The rats likely ruled out any chance of Eileen agreeing to go there for a holiday together. I couldn't risk not telling her and taking her up there so I didn't mention the offer to her at all.

I thanked Harry and said, "We appreciate your offer Harry but we only recently made other plans." This was a little untruth but I thought it the best way to decline Harry's kindness.

Wharf wages started off at £11 for 63 hours in 1954, supplemented with bonuses paid monthly. The bonuses were anywhere from £20 upwards.

With a large workforce employed on the wharfs and with so much manufactured product and produce coming in, it would be unusual to expect to have a total absence of questionable activity. On one occasion I recall finding lamb's legs and ribs in my bag. Were these put there as a case of 'mistaken bag identity' or was the intention to use unsuspecting bag owners to carry the stolen goods out of the wharf confines to be picked up once outside? Whiskey crates, Dinky Toys and razors mentioned earlier and no doubt a number of other goods, illegally obtained, found their way into the outside world.

For 23 years, my typical day began with rising at 5.30 am. Breakfast was a simple toast or two along with a 'cuppa' of tea. Every morning, I would catch the bus on Mt Albert Road. An option was to take the car, but finding parking was a problem and the bus was handy. So it was easier to leave the car at home rather than risk finding parking, or having the car damaged or even stolen. Reporting to the wharf work bureau office at 8 am, workers would be allocated to particular ships. Accusations of favouritism being shown in allocating work were bandied about, however it was a difficult thing to prove. Not hard to believe though, since bonuses and the stresses of some of the work might well have leant itself to unauthorized inducements. Those allocated to the preferred wheat boats received the best bonuses as these boats could be turned around in a shorter time compared to most of the other cargoes. No workers ever enjoyed hearing – wool ship! Work on the bigger boats could take between 10 to 14 days to achieve a turnaround.

No doubt port charges and the length of time taken to turn ships around were the main factors in moving to containerisation and to technical development changes in the ensuing years. Mechanisation had started replacing manual labour. The labour force which at one time numbered some 1700 is just a fraction of that today, while at the same time containerisation and volume has significantly increased. Working a six day week was the norm. These were the days of the 'Sunday dads' when children didn't see their fathers in the morning and were lucky to see them for an hour in the evening. To compensate for this I would often bring home a treat on Friday nights. The three children would eagerly await their bag of jubes, blackballs or liquorice allsorts. For Eileen, chocolate caramels I purchased from downtown Woolworths were in the bag. Lunch was always appreciated on the wharf. Eileen would prepare sardine or salmon sandwiches for me.

When a ship could be loaded and be ready for departure before 10 pm, overtime would be offered as there was no night shift worked. If the job was completed early, the men would still be paid until 10 pm so this was an added inducement. My name always went in the hat when overtime was offered.

However, the usual finishing time for me was 5 pm. My bus would travel along Dominion Road dropping me off at Mt Roskill. The same route I took for 23 years! A short walk along Mt Albert Road and then down a little right-of-way and home to number 7, Milliken Road was the norm. Dinner was at 7 pm, mainly mash and peas with sausage and sometimes steak *(Lou: I remember the same when visiting Sandra, Wednesday nights)*. In the years before television first appeared, evenings were spent listening to the radio and maybe playing some music on our wind up gramophone set. Irvin Berlin tunes were a definite favourite of Eileen's although she didn't have a huge appreciation for musical things. Washing, always needing to be done, wasn't done in temperature controlled automatic washing machines with their fancy jet showers, but in two concrete tubs. The washing when ready, pushed through a good old ringer machine – no fancy tumbler dryers. If hot water was needed it was collected from the kitchen tap. A small copper washer with its own chimney sat in one corner but this just sat there, never used. Did whites come out white? I don't really know as TV advertising hadn't arrived.

Soap, often unbranded sandstone soap, scrubbed skin hard but clean. If dirt did not come off easily you rubbed a little more or used a hard brush. No allowance for 'softies' in those days.

In 1977 after 23 years working at the Ports of Auckland I retired. The National Government at the time under Robert Muldoon had just introduced an early retirement scheme. Coupled with the realisation that a number of my fellow wharfies had suffered heart attacks, the decision was not too difficult to make. I think it creditable that I was never without a job. When jobs were few and far between I went out and found work. I tried my hand at a range of them – process work, farming, painting and finally my long stint on the wharf. Whenever I became disinterested in the work I was doing I would go out and change jobs. Of that I am proud.

My work ethic was one where if there was work available, you worked. You did not hang around until something 'easy' came up. Saying that, work was work, it wasn't my only focus in life. I felt entitled to have just a few vices.

For me whether I deserved it or not, there would be a long and healthy retirement. I was to be lucky indeed!

CHAPTER EIGHT

HOLIDAYS, AUTOMOBILES, THE TAB, FISHING AND CIGARETTES

Gisborne Holidays

Our family holidays were spent in Gisborne, at the Waikanae Motor Camp. In December, every year, after the car was packed, our rather long journey would begin, making stops along the Papamoa/Whakatane coast to stretch the legs. The coffee flask and a biscuit or two came out while the children skipped off to have a run along the beach. Lunch was welcomed but the sandflies were monsters and bit hard. The 60 kilometres or so of the Waioeka Gorge could wear the patience thin. Rock falls threatened through here, rocks once hitting the back of our then Singer Vogue. Once the gorge was cleared, Gisborne soon beckoned and life was good.

    The annual holidays to Gisborne started when the children were young and continued until they left home. After that we didn't go anymore. Gisborne called the Knill family every year and no other holiday resort ever won our custom. Gisborne helped to revitalise our worn bodies. Our holidays were always well planned, starting with the hiring of tents from E. Le Roy in Queen Street. A lot of thought went into packing the car. Making sure we had plenty of cooking pots, an essential. Of the two Gisborne camp site options, we preferred Waikanae Beach Camp to the Churchill Camp located a little further south. The first few holidays were spent in the Le Roy tents, after which we graduated to the luxury of camp cabins.

Gisborne holidays – 1964 – Keith and Eileen

Camp concerts were popular at New Years, more for the young than for the old. Eileen and I were not really into loud music, so we were content to stay in our cabin, leaving the young to their own entertainment.

With Norfolk Pines stretching out along the beach edge and kikuyu grass verges at their base, we accounted for many a day by reading in the shade, or sun tanning on a deck chair.

Responsibilities for cooking and washing jobs were taken in turn and done in the camp facilities. Such was the New Zealand heritage we enjoyed and shared in.

Keen on fishing all my life, I found Gisborne a frustrating spot as far as indulging in this sport goes. Try as I may, with different gear, different bait and every secret fishing spot I could find, no fish ever hooked onto my line! Fish n Chips from the town takeaways was as close as I got to bringing home a fish. The beggars always got the better of me.

Eileen and Sandra at Waikanae Motor Camp tennis courts – 1962

These were the years when New Zealand shut down over the three week Christmas period and many families booked into holiday camps.

Staggered holidays were unheard of.

Waikanae Motor Camp, Gisborne – Keith Knill - 1962

A much longer journey around the East Cape was a variation on the annual trip through the Waioeka Gorge. Beautiful as it was, we only took this route once, mainly for the sightseeing opportunities.

On this trip, memories of salivating taste buds return when recalling how we purchased some fresh salt water crayfish for just half a crown (two shillings and sixpence). Out came the cooking pots, always brought along as part of the holiday packing. Gathering a few river stones, the crayfish went into the pot, the pot was placed onto the stones, the kindling lit, and soon we had the crayfish eaten.

To break such a long journey, stops at the Maori settlement of Te Kaha were sometimes made. Via a princely sum of five shillings, we were able to purchase a tent site and not much else. From a small spring located near the top of a hill, we collected fresh water by channelling it down a long piece of spouting into a bucket at the bottom. Local life, simple as it was, observed as Maori rode horses along the beach. The best life might well be the simple life.

Visits to Australia

Eileen and I did not travel extensively. We never visited the South Island although there was the intention to do so, nor did we ever tour around the North Island. We never journeyed to Wanganui to visit Lorraine and Ray. Expressing a wish to visit the South Island and actually getting in the car and going can be chalk and cheese apart. Eileen would say,

"Look at us, the kids have all visited the South Island but not us."

Anticipating her frustration I would say, "I can go and book the bus if you want to go."

"No, we wouldn't know what to do."

A wish not materialised for us, more than likely because the hassle of preparing and getting there outweighed everything else. Also I was aware that Eileen suffered from a form of claustrophobia whenever she found herself in confined spaces or in crowded situations.

The furthest travel we undertook was to see our son Len and Bev and grandchildren, Cherie and Robbie, on the Gold Coast in Australia. Laden with pockets full of coins, destined for Gold Coast pokies, we must have exceeded our baggage weight limits before we even had our bags weighed. Frequent flyers as we were, we visited Australia five times, staying approximately two weeks each time. Early trips were to Len and Bev's home at Burleigh Heads where Len managed the White Horse Apartments.

The Terranora Golf Club in Terranora, about 45 minutes south of Burleigh Heads, offered champagne and bacon and egg breakfasts. Breakfast was free when Len and Bev took us on an outing there. Encouraged by a healthy start to the day an investment or two at the pokie machines was a natural follow up. Bev was the only lucky one, however, like she said, she only won enough to buy a bus ticket half way home. Len usually gave back his initial winnings plus a little extra.

We loved going down to the bowls club and waiting for Len to finish work, which he would do at about 1 pm if he knew we were coming into town to meet him. Eileen would go and buy all of them a chocolate éclair then go down to the TAB for a flutter. After our day in town, it was home for a few drinks and tea. Eileen kept a little bottle of gin in her bedroom. Of course she would insist it was for medicinal purposes, a claim she made consistently. We would not argue with her. Watching TV in the evening may have been part of everyone else's plan but they tell me that I loved to talk, and I suppose I did (as I have always done), so nothing new in that. Did I really stop everyone from watching TV?

Nan and Pop in Australia with Len, Robbie and Cherie – late 70s.

Eileen and I thought Australian beaches were 'clean', especially after seeing beach cleaning machines sieving the sand to catch dog droppings and other contaminates.

Jupiter's Casino, 500 yards from the Pacific Fair Shopping Centre and half an hour north of Burleigh Heads was another of our favourite gambling haunts. Of multi story proportions, its bright lights and cascading waterfalls beckoned customers to come in and see more. Fun was had but winning did not happen too often. At least we all got a bit of a buzz seeing and hearing coins tumbling out of machines – only it wasn't ours. Still being a gambling man, I live in hope, of one day?

A recollection from one of our visits from Len's wife Bev goes like this;

"Just another thing I remember, when Mum and Dad came over one year, Pop forgot to pack his pants and he only had the pants he was wearing on the plane over and they were his big thick woolly pants and he got too hot in them, anyway we were taking them to the Seagulls Rugby League Club for a meal and a flutter on the pokies and Dad said he would be too hot in his pants, so Mum made him wear a pair of her slacks, he was so embarrassed but put them on. Once we got there and had our meal and had a flutter, we sat down by the band and watched the people dancing. Anyway Dad needed to go and have a wee and he came back so embarrassed as he had to pull his pants down at the urinal to go. Then he sits down, explaining to us, and we are all laughing our heads off and some girl comes up to him and asks him for a dance. Poor Dad nearly fell through the floor, he was trying to be so inconspicuous in a pair of ladies slacks and here he is being dragged onto the floor, we just couldn't stop laughing. It was a very good night!"

The girls loved to have a look around the shops together. Shopping was surprisingly risk free, apart from when Cherrie sought out the latest fashion shorts. When Cherie took Nan in tow, the hours whisked on by.

While thousands enjoy swimming in the renowned Gold Coast surf it was something Len said that put me off,

"Go and have a swim, dad, it's quite safe and the shark nets are up, there is the odd hole in them but the sharks won't see the holes anyway."

"Yeah, thanks Len."

Swimming did not appeal so much after that. My swimming trunks were left untouched in my bag.

Conveniently situated in the centre of Burleigh Heads, the TAB happily took New Zealand investments. A quinella I struck of near $90 on one visit almost matched my biggest collect ever. Len looked at my ability to select race winners differently after that win. Since then I think I remember him asking me a few times, "Who do you like in this one dad?"

That was not something he had asked me before. Mind you, I have been known to have put him crook on a few occasions.

Evening meals at the casino and pies from local pie shops were the norm when we didn't eat in. Eileen and I voted the Australian pies to be just a little healthier and more sophisticated that the New Zealand cousins.

We would have visited Australia more often but for the fact that on our third visit to Australia Eileen suffered an angina attack while flying in to the airport. Len had gone to Brisbane airport to pick us up while Bev prepared dinner at home. When we got home Eileen went straight upstairs. Bev went up and realised the seriousness of the situation and she made an instant decision to take Eileen to the doctors. The doctor advised us to go straight to the hospital and that it would be quicker if Len and Bev took her in their station wagon. We drove into the ambulance bay at Gold Coast Hospital where the medical team was waiting. Most of the holiday was spent at the hospital. I cried a lot then. Len would try to create some diversion by taking me to the TAB located just down the road. Eileen's dislike of hospitals and people fussing over her dampened her enthusiasm for further visits. This would be the first of a series of attacks she was to suffer over the following years.

Automobiles

You can't tell a man's story without talking about a man's cars. Prized and loved, cleaned and polished, oil and greased, they got lots of attention. The kilometres they travelled I counted and compared when talking to others about cars. For Eileen, the car provided her with the means to get away from the house, to travel up to the shops. Proud when a new car came into the family, Eileen would feel secure in the fact that neighbours recognised a new car as a rise in status. That meant a lot to her.

Ford Model A Roadster

This was the first car I purchased while working for the Railways at Maungaturoto. She needed to be started by setting the spark gap and giving it a good old crank with the crank handle. The Ford made me a popular man up north.

Ford Anglia

She was the model with two doors. The Anglia was not with us for long as it was a hassle fitting in the kids. The car was painted a vegetable green and she was purchased second hand. This was a late 1950s model.

While the Model A had to be started with a good old crank, when the car battery came along that task was eliminated. Now all we had to do was regularly check all the battery cells and top them up with water.

The Majestic car battery made by Australasian Battery Co Ltd - New Zealand's largest battery firm, 1939. (Source: www.completestamp.co.nz – 151058)

Morris Minor

The 'Morrie' –stopping for something to eat – Opotiki – back from Gisborne holidays – 1962.

The second in the fleet was a grey Morris Minor. These models were the ones with the rounded profiles, rust proof models of the early 1950s. At one shilling and nine pence a gallon, petrol wasn't much of a concern. The 'Morrie' was a reliable vehicle. She did the annual Gisborne holiday trip and the 'long one' around the East Cape with ease.

Morris 1100

This car happened to be a yellow one, a colour not so common at the time. Its claim to fame was being the first model to have hydraulic (hydrolastic) suspension. She also did the Gisborne trip a few times. More loved than the Minor.

Singer Vogue

We purchased her from Shorters of Shorthand Street Motors. The Singer had an ignition problem, but Shorters' warranty didn't cover this. Customer service departments might well be a little more generous in today's world. She had a little more power at 1800cc. The Singer was traded in for the Mitsubishi. Eileen always worried about the car's petrol consumption.

The Singer Vogue – at Millbrook Road, Henderson, 1974.

Mitsubishi Lancer

Ah! The brown Mitsubishi purchased from the showroom floor of Greenlane Motors. Eileen saw it and wanted it. The day the 'Mitsi' came into the family was one of the happiest days of Eileen's life. The day it could no longer take her places, due to me losing my licence, equalled the most depressing day of Eileen's life.

Nan with her pride and joy – then!

We always kept this car in immaculate condition. For most of its life, we drove it maybe once a week and if lucky twice a week. After its outing, the car was driven into the garage, wiped and covered lovingly with a full cover cloth. We owned our shiny brown Mitsi for 40 years, travelling in it a total of 40,000 kms. Bruce, the neighbour, joked when it rained, that the car wouldn't be out today. Purchased for $5,000 it was sold for the bargain price of $1,000.

Our cars were lovingly cared for. They never saw a service station unless in an emergency. I did all the oil and greases myself.

Horses, The TAB and Cigarettes

Most of us have a passion in life which provides us with an interest and with some excitement. For Eileen and me, the ritual of spreading out the Best Bets, noting dots and scribbles besides our selected horses or jockeys was more than a common sight. The radio or transistor switched on to hear the early morning scratchings. Choices were finalised and it was off to the TAB. Later developments such as phone betting never caught on with us, and walking up to the TAB remained a traditional habit we enjoyed.

Early Saturday morning at the TAB. (Source: NZ History – University Of Auckland)

We tried many schemes and systems, some dreamt up by ourselves, others offered by so called experts as almost foolproof. None of them worked. Fortunes were never made. My greatest collect from memory was $90. Some might say that putting so much effort into selecting winners and not making any money is not worth it, but for us, enjoyment cannot be measured solely by a positive return on the financial investment. It never was. Eileen seemed to have more luck than I did. Whereas I took a conservative approach to my betting, often taking Trackside host Mike Dillon's picks, usually a $1 place or win bet, Eileen was much more adventurous splashing out occasionally on a 'field' bet. She was sometimes secretive about her TAB accounts. It transpired upon her passing that stashes of TAB winnings had been 'banked' into home accounts, located or hidden in secret hideouts. The enjoyment gained from 'investing' brought many a joy for Eileen and me, and for us was irreplaceable.

Now I can bring cigarette smoking into the story here – why here? – maybe because it's as good a place to start as any. Cigarette smoking has been a life-long pastime, (at least since being introduced to it), habit and enjoyment for me. This addiction of mine had to start somewhere and the blame has to be laid at the foot of the army. Being issued with 'cigs' to alleviate periods of boredom out in the desert, surrounded by the harsh environment of war, seemed a natural thing to do and anyway I thought I could easily die out there. Smoking certainly did not carry with it the health warnings of today. Movies of the day regularly showed leading ladies and gentlemen lighting up. I would describe the flavour of our war time issues of English cigarettes as 'mouldy' and the 'Cape de Cairos' of Egypt as made of 'horseshit'. The taste of these things made me believe the cigs had been stored in dungeons. Whatever they were made of, smoke them I did. My habit had begun. A vice had taken hold of me.

'Camels' not 'Cape de Cairo's' but you might think Camels were made for desert smoking. (Sources: Soldier – http-wellmedicated.com-52; Fresh – Vintage America – 4141762701))

In those days the harmful health effects of tobacco were not yet fully understood. But judging by my performance in being alive and kicking at 96, and still rolling my own to this day, all the medical professions warnings about the dangers seem to have been defied. The medical fraternity may wish to do a case study on me and send me to the lab for further exploratory study.

I don't think choosing Christmas presents for me would ever have posed anyone a problem – a packet of Roll Your Own and cigarette paper made me happy. Should anyone deny me this pleasure? It has not shortened my life unless I was destined to live to 120. I enjoy nothing better than rolling a cig and sitting down to have a chat. In my 96th year I have decided to cut back, a self-imposed restriction to six or seven max a day. Why have I suddenly got tough on myself? I don't know really - put it down to another unexplained mystery.

Fishing

All around the world fishing is a sport and a livelihood for millions of people. I think many of those would have been introduced to fishing at a young age, as I was, when father took me fishing, down at the Auckland waterfront. I was 'hooked' so to say, in my boyhood. Holidays in Gisborne saw me trying to catch fish where fish were very hard, if not impossible to catch. I always started off with high expectations of catching something. Optimism is a necessary attitude which all fishermen should connect with.

Fishing in my retirement years brought many pleasures. There were many days spent strolling up Florence Ave, fishing gear in hand, to Orewa Beach. There is something about fishing that true fishermen have and which can be difficult to explain to non-fishermen. There is the beauty and mystique of the ocean, changing its nature every day. Then there is the uncertainty of the catch and what you might catch. Be you successful or unsuccessful, both draw you back even more determined.

In my later years I was lucky enough to have a keen fisherman, Neville Wright, move in as our next door neighbour. Neville was a very friendly chap who could talk for hours. Eileen didn't mind him either and she realised he and I enjoyed common interests, especially fishing. We struck up a friendship and spent many hours together throwing out lines at Orewa Beach. When Neville invested a few thousand dollars in a motorised kon-tiki he got quite exited and I remember him saying, "Charlie, you don't need to worry any more, life will be easy with this. All we need to do now is launch, wait, and pull in the fish."

"Do you think we will be able to work the thing?" I questioned.

Neville was obviously confident. I went with it.

Well, it wasn't quite like that. Mechanical problems, entanglements, ill winds, even seagulls stuffed things up on occasions. You couldn't say the new gadget provided hassle free entertainment. Our pioneering spirits, as old as we were, helped us enjoy this interlude of our lives.

I spent many days holding hands with the ocean, patiently waiting for a catch that many a time never happened. The catches were celebrated with joy, the misses just made me more determined to come back and try again. If I didn't catch them, they were still there.

During fifty years of working, starting in a hat factory, then four or more years farming, five years on the Railways, three years in the army, then painting around Auckland city and finally working a long stint within the confines of the Auckland wharfs, I always managed to stay employed. I enjoyed simple pleasures in life, including pleasures that some might frown upon such as smoking and gambling.

Does anyone know how many years of retirement they may be granted? Would the lessons I learnt during my working life and the joys I obtained from my simple pleasures sustain me in my retirement years? I was going to find out because my retirement was going to be a long one.

CHAPTER NINE

RETIREMENT

After my long service at the wharf, I retired in 1977. Thirty four years of retirement is a generous allocation of years – a lot longer than many get to experience. For me certainly, retirement has never meant sitting in an arm chair and putting my feet up.

    I have never been one to sit still, and tasks of all descriptions have kept me occupied for all of those 34 years. Many a lawnmower blade has been worn out; many blades have been sharpened. Many a mower repaired, pulled apart and stuck back together again. The car was often in the garage but it still had to have oil changes and be cleaned. Gardening has always been a hobby. From the unsuccessful banana growing exercise in Milliken Road to the water logged spuds in Florence Avenue, gardening has occupied many of my days and brought me much pleasure. Always a topic of conversation, many a day on the back porch has been spent discussing gardening problems. Tomatoes and potatoes, beans and cucumbers took much of my time when I went into the vegetable garden. They were my favourites. The two poplar trees which continually shed their leaves, invading the vegetable patch with unwelcome leafage were the subject of many an extermination plan that Eileen and I pondered over. The enormous Norfolk pine which stood tall and proud in a corner at the back of the section, was also included in possible extermination discussions.

This was the tree visitors to our humble abode set their Orewa bearings on as soon as they arrived at the end of the North Western motorway. Look right and there it was. Better than a traffic sign when trying to locate our place. The tuis loved it, using its branches as a launching pad to invade the neighbouring flax plants. For Eileen and I, the threat of the thing falling down on our house, negated any warm feelings we had for its domineering beauty. Every storm predicted on TV news weather, meant we had to think about the height and root structure of that forever growing Norfolk Pine.

The Norfolk pine sitting proud at the back of the section flanked by the two poplars on the right.

The two poplars which stood beside it were another cause for concern, especially after a friendly visitor suggested that the trees or their branches were at risk of falling onto our garage roof. Little did the kind visitor realise that such a comment, made with all the caring in the world, would sow the seeds of panic in our nervous minds. It took many years before a solution came, when in early 2012 a council consent was received allowing the poplars to be trimmed. I didn't want them 'killed', I only wanted to eliminate the risk of them toppling on to our garage or on to our neighbour's property. Having them chopped in half would have satisfied me.

Back view from the sports ground – the two poplars and the Norfolk pine

Both the vegetable patch and the flower gardens were given much attention. We realised that our colourful flowers gave joy to many a neighbour who passed by. Always proudly 'presented' by Eileen, aware of the standing a beautiful garden had in the community, and recognised by many townsfolk as they strolled by. Flowers, plants, Latin names, disease, growing conditions, spacing and groupings all required careful contemplation and sorting out. If life ever came to a standstill I could always skip outside and into the garden.

Having the local sports ground located just beyond our back yard meant that Eileen and I could participate as sideline spectators as competitions and practices were held.

Living in the Hibiscus Coast area in Orewa, we had the sea as our next door neighbour. On a quiet day we could hear waves breaking on the shore. When the children and grandchildren visited, seaside outings were a must, otherwise we would have experienced mutinies. Eileen and I tagged along with children and grandchildren as we all ambled up to the beach. We would bring along a picnic basket or stop off at Saigon Bakery for ready-made goodies. Selecting a spot at the northern end of the beach, the umbrella went up, and while adults chatted away, grandchildren jumped into the ocean and swum for hours.

'The Beach' gave Eileen and I and our children and their children so much.

At holiday time, tents were pitched up on the lawn under the Norfolk Pine and on other occasions, the garage provided a holiday cabin. Family holiday-makers shared the garage with the car, lawnmower and washing machine. Card games, holiday radio, sleeping bags and Saigon pies (there's that name again) decorated our outbuilding. There were no complaints to the management. We loved having family spend time with us. Happiness is infectious.

'The Spot' pretty much opposite Florence Ave, where we spent many enjoyable hours picnicking, chatting, fishing, swimming and more.

Eileen loved lawn bowls and there is no doubt it was one of the loves of her life. She played many a game and played well. Eileen possessed a very competitive spirit, enjoying the heat of battle. Having a 'roll up' never really appealed to her. At the bowling club she got on well with her fellow bowlers. Bowling functions and prize giving's were looked forward to and eagerly participated in. The day Eileen entered Greenlane Hospital for a triple bypass heart operation was, as the song *American Pie* says, 'the day the music died'. It frustrated Eileen that she could no longer play competitively. She kept in touch with the Orewa bowling club for a while, attending functions, but nothing could match the buzz she got from playing. Sometime after Eileen joined the Orewa club, I also became a member. I did not possess the same competitive spirit which Eileen did, however it was a pleasure being at the club, especially enjoying the social atmosphere. I reckon I put down a few good bowls myself.

Tennis, played at Maungaturoto all those years ago, has been a fond memory of mine. A sport I have always enjoyed. I recall on a visit to Rotorua in 1998, playing a game at the FRI courts in Sala Street, Lou at one end and myself at the other. I made him do some running according to Lou, who told me he did more of it than I did. If that is the truth, I am happy with that, since many men of 84 would have difficulty collecting their mail from the letter box.

Our televisions, favourites in the entertainment stakes, sat - one in a corner of the lounge and the second in the bedroom. Trackside, Coronation Street, Emmerdale Farm and sports always captured our interest and attention. There weren't too many arguments over the remote (which we got to know only in later years) as we both liked the same programmes and sport. Still, there were the personal favourites that each had, whether it be a particular horse or race meeting, a favourite rugby team or favourite player. Eileen watched rugby with keen interest, especially when Jimmy Cowan played. We kept things simple, video players, computers and digital washing machines confused the daylights out of us, and for all we cared, these modern gadgets could stay on the shelves in the electrical appliance stores.

Eileen retired to bed mostly at 8.30 pm, or after watching her favourite Coronation Street. Usually a little early for me as I would stay up a little later, switching the TV off at 9.30 and then dialling in to radio talkback. I happened to be a bit of a night owl. After Eileen was gone, in December 2011, many an evening lingered on to 10.30 pm or up to midnight talking on the telephone. Telephone calls continuing on till after 10 pm were never a problem.

Not really being into music, there was no CD or record player in our home. Apart from Julie Andrews' 'The Sound of Music' songs, tunes from Irving Berlin, the National Anthem and 'Peace in the Valley,' which were a few of the tunes Eileen enjoyed, music did not really feature as a keen interest of ours.

A fond memory of Eileen which will always be missed is the regular Sunday phone calls. These always had a mix of laughter and concern and never a call went by without an enquiry as to what was going on in the children's lives. Discussing and sharing sport and racing trivia added to the fun of the telephone conversations.

"How is Lou's mum?" or "How are the children doing?" being typical questions. Every now and then the laughter sounded just that little bit more vigorous and louder, put down to the partaking of a little gin. Medicinal purposes of course - lovely anyway!

The long retirement that Eileen and I had lived together was about to change forever.

At 96 and definitely not solely dependent on a mobility scooter - with great grandson Josh.

CHAPTER 10

THE MORE RECENT YEARS - POP'S LEGACY, NAN

By Lou Geraets

Through the first decades of the 21st Century, life continued. It was in Rotorua in 2011 where much of this story unfolded. Sixty seven years of marriage lived together; most of it doing their thing in the little cottage at 91 Florence suddenly came to an end on the 23rd August 2011. Pop believing that it didn't need to be, shouldn't have been, and wishing only for another five more years with Eileen and then she could have gone. Why it was five years and not four or six years, I am not sure of.

Grieving takes many a different form; loss, denial, anger and sadness are but some of them. Acceptance seems to be the last emotion that is dealt with in this process. Pop experienced them all. It surprised many when the house was transformed. Out went dolls, mats and sheepskins, and clocks and more clocks, not because they didn't fit but because if they were gone maybe Eileen's memories would not come flooding back. Pop found them painful to recall and wanted to be able to delay them until he was again ready to let them flow back. Garage sales and grandchildren benefited. Two or three gin bottles were found. Eileen was known to partake of the odd nip or two. It transpired that the gin bottles were kept in the house rather than be delivered to the roadside rubbish collection. There was no way that Eileen was going to risk a neighbourhood security camera or roving eye discovering one of her private enjoyments. Good on her anyway for taking on the odd personal pleasure. Just sits so well in painting a picture of dear old Nan. Medicinal purposes of course!

Pop was paralysed, flitting from one emotion to another. Keith (younger son) and wife Christine became aged caregivers in more ways than one. The practicalities had to be taken care of, meals, arrangements and many things more. Most of all they became counsellors, listening to many a soulful cry. Big brother Len flew over from Australia and became house manager and a shoulder to cry on until arrangements were made for Pop to spend three weeks recovery time with Sandra and her family in Rotorua.

Travelling through the various stages of grieving, whatever routes it takes, cannot be easy and no magic recipe exits for grief's release. For Pop it was tough. Sixty seven years of marriage suddenly coming to its end, elicits a response. There were some interesting reactions; things disappearing, denials, a variety of emotional expressions, clairvoyant projections and starvations. Many a passing neighbour offered an answer to Pop's questioning of, "How long does it take?" Some suggested that grieving never ends, others suggested that it could take six years. Pop asked that question many times but he never did get the answer he was looking for.

Losing your partner leaves the survivor recollecting memories of days gone by. Memories brought back by predictable and unpredictable events in any particular day, like finding Nan's favourite mug, seeing the tear in the lounge curtain, hearing the clock chime (any one of many clocks which adorned the lounge), remembering comments Nan made about the pictures hung in the lounge or seeing her favourite flower again when going out to check on the mail. Pop felt he had little control over, when, or how often these memories would suddenly come over him. Feeling like he was, he didn't want to remember anything about Eileen - sweet or sad. But unable to switch off these memories as they came and went, he got stuck on what he felt were certain unresolved issues, things Pop thought he could have changed had he been given another five years with Eileen. These thoughts kept coming back and he didn't want them to!

One, recanted more than once, involved the 'photographs incident'. Eileen had apparently said something to Pop to the effect that 'I don't care about those photos', which Pop took to mean that they could disappear somewhere (what was he thinking of?). He took the photographs out to the garage and put them in the garbage can. Eileen understandably became most upset by this. An action that Pop has regretted to this day and wishes he could retract.

One more mystery to add to the mix!

Looking back all those years, one can feel something of the sense of being a 'loner' that Pop carried with him. In Maungaturoto, in England, Egypt and in Tripoli, the loner in him led him to spend nights on his own or with a few mates out in the open. When Eileen passed away he was alone again. He had made what he calls 'a spur of the moment' proposal 67 years ago. He had not regretted it, but wondered how much more of a true 'loner' he could have been.

His steely determination must have played a major part in his long marriage and long life. If you can summarise a life, how would you summarise Pop's? There is much to be proud of. Many sacrifices selflessly made. An open mind always attentive to the company in his presence. Did he accept his lot? What were his thoughts when he said "In those days, like at Maungaturoto, we worked from 6 to 3 with Bill Hickey and the lads and then we went to the pub? We enjoyed ourselves, but look at me now – I'm just a jelly and without Eileen?"

And then he got up, made another cup of tea and started to think about what to do next.

CHAPTER 11

FINAL WORDS

There are many ways to remember a loved one's life; photo albums, video recordings, letters, cards, stories and others. Writing down the whole story covering almost 100 years is a richly rewarding exercise. Details that would never have been told are captured, painting pictures in the mind. When one has known the loved one for so long, you come to believe that you know most things about the person. How wrong you can be.

Piecing together the events that shaped Pop's life, discussing and questioning his thinking and behaviour helps us to look deeper into the joys, tribulations and aspirations of his long life. We are fortunate indeed to be able to walk alongside our father and grandfather, appreciating a tapestry of a human life lived.

You will not find Pop's life chronicled in New Zealand libraries, nor see him in portraits adorning RSA walls, no mention on the New Zealand Honours list of recipients and definitely not found on New Zealand's rich list. For Pop, achieving any of these things would not have made him a better man and wouldn't have changed much in this story. No magical answers dive out at us from these pages in reply to some of Pop's deeper thinking and the questions he asked about life. Not all questions have been answered and they needn't be and it's probably true that we shall ponder things further. However we can be grateful to have gained an insight into Pop's own personal story.

Respect comes from an admiration for this life, for being true to himself, for never being interested in projecting success based on social elegances. Respect need never be gauged from the numbers attending his final burial.

Through the writing down of this life there has never been any attempt to paint up a high profile life, to justify decisions made or to create falsehoods. It is what it is. It is what you read here in these pages.

It has been a privilege and a reward to share hours of conversation and scribbled notes and to reflect on so many stories and insights of Charlie Knill's meanderings.

It is a story that is not going to die, for Pop – we won't forget.

ABOUT THE AUTHOR

Lou W Geraets was born in Venlo, Holland in 1949. Lou never wanted life to just roll on by. After his father-in-law, Charlie Knill, dreamed of telling his life story, Lou picked up a pen and started to write. He lives with his family and a few farm animals in Rotorua, New Zealand, and works as a business systems co-ordinator.

INDEX

2nd NZ Echelon, 63, 69, 80, 110
3rd NZ Division, Japanese, Green Island, 16, 138
3ZM, 1YA, 40
4th Brigade, 88, 106-107, 139
5th Infantry Brigade, 5th Field Regiment, 63, 85, 107, 111
7th Anti-Tank Regiment (31&32 Batteries), 63
7th Armoured Division, 118, 125
7th Field (Engineer) Company, 63
7 Millikin Road, Mt Roskill 151, 154, 161, 167, 185
21st, 22nd, 28th Maori Infantry Battalion, 63-64
91 Florence Avenue, Orewa, 16, 183, 185, 188, 191

Abbott, Armstrong & Howie, Albert St, 33
Adams Bruce, 2
Aldershot, London, Coventry, 67-68, 139
Alexandria, 74, 78, 95, 112, 115
Aliakmon Line, 83
Anglo Canadian (ship), 81
Anzac Ave, 25
Aquitania, 63-67, 76
Armstrong, Hubert Thomas (Tim), Minister of Labour, 45
Athens, 81
Auchinleck, General Claude (Field Marshal Sir), 106
Auckland, 1-3, 11-13, 16, 22, 31, 33, 41-42, 45, 50-52, 60, 89, 135, 138, 149, 156, 162, 164, 184
    and Greyhound Club, 149
    and Town Hall, 26
    and Auckland Star, 156
Auckland Wharfs, Ports, 12-13, 16, 89, 158, 161-165, 168, 183
    and The Tofua, Oriana, Mariposa, 163-164
    and Waterfront Strike, 1951, 161
Australian Bight – Perth – Bass Straight, 135
Australian Forces, 80, 98, 105-106, 118
Australia, Gold Coast, Burleigh Heads, 155, 161, 163, 172-175

Beachlands, 25-26
Beesley Annie, Billy & Owen, 4-10, 12, 15-16, 19-20, 25, 28, 30, 33, 34, 53, 135-138
Beesley, Edie, 5, 12, 15, 137
Best, John – Bren Carriers – ex-All Black, 84

Bishop Averil, 5th Anglican Bishop of Auckland, 11
Blanford Park, 25
Blomfield, Lofty, 26
Box, Cyril, Department of Railways, 45, 60
Bracegirdle, Jim, 58
Braithwaite, Augustus, 3
Bren Carriers and Guns, 69, 79, 81, 83-86, 100, 105, 122-124, 128
Britain, 57, 63, 83, 98
British and Commonwealth Forces, 81, 105
Butland Industries, 13, 36

C Squadron of the Divisional Cavalry, 63, 124
Cairo, 70, 72-75, 102, 116-117
      and Cape de Cairos 181
Cameo Picture Theatre, 2
Cape Town, South Africa, 63, 65
Chappell, Jim– husband of Alma and Trevor and Pat (children), 13
Chinaman's Hill, 1-3
Church of Christ, Newton, Karangahape Road, 35
Churchill Camp, 169
Churchill, Winston, 80, 87, 100, 120
Clansman, The (ship), 41
Compensation Court, 36
Cowley Family – Mark, Thead, Tom, 37
Corinth, 86-89, 91, 92
Crete, 90-95, 105
Crystal Palace, Pat McMinn, Epi Shalfoon Band, 15, 141
Cummings, Bart, 54

Debey, Don, 58
Depression, Great, NZ, 2, 25, 30-31, 33, 35-36, 44
Divisional Cavalry, 63, 100, 107, 111, 121
Duchess of Bedford, 69

East Cape, North Island, 172
Easter Show, Epsom Showground, 27
Eastwood, Clint – The Good, the Bad and the Ugly, 44
Edinburgh, Scotland, 68
Egypt, 53, 63-64, 67-70, 75-80, 90-91, 93-97, 100, 102-103, 105–108, 112, 118, 124, 129, 134-135, 137, 143, 181, 193
Eighth Army, 118, 121, 123, 134
El Alamein, 110-113, 117-120, 124
El E Acman, 86

Elements of the 6th Brigade HQ, 63, 106
Ellis, Bruce, 161
England, 1, 64-65, 67, 69, 79, 97-98, 124, 139, 145, 151, 159, 163, 193
Evans Family, Con & Nan (Ettie), Lorraine, Edwin, Daphne, Ron, 15, 76, 142, 144-146, 148-150, 160, 172

Fairburn, A.R.D. – NZ Poet – Note on NZR, 46
Farmers, Hobson Street, 25, 153
Fiji, 14
Fishing – Gisborne, Orewa Beach, 16, 25, 169, 170, 183
Foodtown, Countdown, 56
Ford Model A, Ford Anglia, 176
Fremantle, 64
Freyberg, Major General Bernard, 63, 70, 105

Geraets, Claudine, David, Kim, Michael & Karen, 156
Germany, 58, 82-83, 98-99, 163
Gisborne – Waikanae Motor Camp, Waioeka Gorge, 169-170, 172, 178, 183
Gold Coast Hospital, 175
Golding, Gladys; John, and Maria, 1
Government Training Centres, 159
Grafton Primary School, 18-28
Greece, 30, 34, 80-84, 87, 89-93, 95, 97, 99-100, 105-106, 124, 135
Green Island, Pacific Islands, Solomons, Treasury Islands, 16, 138
Greenlane Hospital, 148, 189
    and Greenlane Motors, 179
Grey, Sir George, 2
Grey, Zane – Riders of the Purple Sage, The last of the Plainsmen, 43
Gribblehurst Park, 23
Grummer, Thomas – Sunny Hills Farms, 2
Gunn, Dennis, 3

Halfaya Pass, 120, 122-123, 125
Halifax bomber, 58
Haresnapes, 154
Helensville, 24
Hellfire Jack, 122-123
Helwan, Bab-el-Louk (railway stations), 73
Hickey, Pat – Railway shunter, Maungaturoto, 48, 57-58
    and Bill, 193
Hikutaia (Thames), 41-43, 158

Hitler, Adolph, 81, 98, 120
HMS Isis – British destroyer, 91-92
Hollis, Mr (first name unknown), 34
Huntly, 47

Innes Jewellers, Queen Street, 143
Irvine, Jim (Mercer Rail), 47
Italian Forces, 67, 105, 119, 120, 122-124, 134

Jury, Norman – boarder, 145

Kensington Park, Whangarei, 59
Knill Family, 1, 22, 27-28, 33, 139, 154, 169
    and Knill, Alma, 4-5, 13-14, 16, 36, 139
    and Ernie, 12, 14-15, 24, 27, 36-37, 40-41, 51, 139, 143, 145, 146
    and Jack, 4, 12-17, 36, 139, 143
    and Irene, 5, 13-14, 16, 36, 139
    and Knill, Charles Alfred Abraham and Alice Eliza (nee Arruis), 1
    and Knill, Cherie, Robbie & Bev, 155, 172-175
    and Knill, Dennis, 15
    and Knill, Eileen, 15, 17, 76, 142-145, 147, 149-157, 166-167, 170, 172-176, 178-181, 183, 185-187, 189
    and Knill, Keith & Christine and Stephen & Katrina, Knill, Len, Keith, Sandra, 140, 150, 154, 156, 167, 192
Khyber Pass, and Khyber Pass Skating Rink, 22, 25, 76, 144
Klidi Pass, Battle of the, (see also the Battle of Vevi) 83, 85-86

Lord Haw Haw – William Joyce, 98, 135
Maadi Camp, 70-73, 77, 79, 87, 90, 96, 99-100, 102-103, 108, 112, 120, 134-135
Mackay Force (Australian, British, NZ), 85
Makarau, 57
Marist Brothers, Vermont St. Brother Calixtus, 28-30
Martin, Mr & Mrs, 152
Mason, Jim, 58
Maungaturoto, 47-53, 55-59, 61-62, 113, 144, 158, 176, 189, 193
Mediterranean, 81, 92, 95, 120, 134
Mercer, 45-48, 52-54, 73, 158
Messerschmitt Bf 109, 88

Metaxas Line, 86
Mitsubishi Lancer, 179
Montgomery, (Field Marshal) Bernard, 118-119, 134
Morris Minor, Morris 1100, Singer Vogue, 169, 178
Mount Olympus, 83

New Zealand Army, 58, 62, 80, 121
New Zealand Club, Cairo, 70
New Zealand Division, 63, 80-81, 86, 105-106, 112, 118-120, 134
New Zealand Expeditionary Force, 63-64, 138
New Zealand Herald, 33, 36-37, 41-42, 156
New Zealand Railways, 45, 48, 51-52, 60, 158-159, 176, 184
Nieuw Amsterdam, 135
North African Campaign, Operation Crusader, 80, 105-106, 112, 118, 124
Nugent Street, 28

Otorohanga, 37, 39, 43

Paeroa-Kopu Road, 41
Papakura Army Base, 62-63, 79-100
Panehoe, Win, 89
Parnell, 23,
    and Parnell Baths, 25
Phillips & Impey, 11
Pop, 3-4, 17, 19, 29, 31, 59, 66, 105, 133, 157, 174, 191-195
    and Pop's Events Book, 66, 113, 123,
    129
    and Pop's Medals, 134
    and Pop's Timeline, 67
Port Greenock – Clyde, 67
Port Piraeus, 81
Port Said, 135
Port Tewfik, 135
Pyramids, Egypt, 71, 102

Queen Street, 25, 143, 169

Ramillies (British), 66
Red Beach, 16
Riverhead, 50
River View Private Hotel. Tom Sunnex, daughters Joan & Betty, 47
Rodgers, Ken, 138

Romania, 81
Rommel, General Field Marshal Erwin, 96, 106-107, 119-120
Rossiter, Dr (first name unknown), 12

Sahara, 100
St Benedict's School, 28
St David's, Church of England, Khyber Pass, 144
Savage, Michael Joseph, PM of NZ, 45, 57, 61
Semple, Bob, Minister of Public Works, 12
Scharnhorst (German cruiser), 66
Seagulls Rugby League Club, 174
Senussi, 125
Shaddock Street, Mt Eden, 12, 15, 18, 20-21, 108, 137-139, 141, 145
Shamrock Hotel, 33
Sidi Bishr, 91, 95, 98-99
Sidi Haneish, 120, 126
Sidi Rezeg, 106-107, 111-112, Belhamed, 106-107 Bardia, 107, 111, Cyrenaica, 107, Libya, 105-108, 118 Baggush, 106, 110, Sollum, 107, 111, 120
Silverdale & Orewa Bowling Clubs, 15
Simpson, Frank, 160
Sister Bertle, 28
Sonny Jims – (Marshmallow Bar), 36
Stuka fighter plane, German, 86
Surrey Crescent, Grey Lynn, 1, 2
Table Mountain (South Africa), 65
Takanini, 42-44
Te Awamutu (Dairy Company), 39
Territorial Army Group, 59-60
Thessalonica, 85
Thurland Castle (ship), 94
Tivoli, The picture theatre, 143
Tobruk, 160
Tripoli, 113, 125, 127-129, 132-134, 193
Tru, Len, 76-77
Turnock Family, Symonds Street, 21
Tutuki Street, 151
Tura Caves (pyramids, Egypt), 102

Vevi, Battle of (or Klidi Pass), 83, 86

Waipa River, 39
Wakeland, Mavis, 52

Wairiki Road, Mt Eden, 145-148, 151, 154, 160
Wayne, John, 44
Wellesley Street, 25
Wellington, 63-64, 77, 135, 137, 139
and Wellington Cup, 149
Western Springs Speedway, 26
Whangarei, 55, 58-60, 108
Williamson, James, 2
Wirth Bros Circus, Australia, 23
Woolley family, 14
    and Woolley, Joyce (wife of Ernie Knill) from Army Bay & Dennis and Maureen, their children, 14-15, 143, 145-146
World Wars, 65
World War I, 1, 105
World War II, 57
Wright, Gathern – Matamata, 39
Wright, Neville – Orewa, 183

Yugoslavia, 83

www.ingramcontent.com/pod-product-compliance
Lightning Source LLC
Chambersburg PA
CBHW061301110426
42742CB00012BA/2005